The Exceptional Child in the Regular Classroom

CORWIN
PRESS

The Corwin Press logo—a raven striding across an open book—represents the happy union of courage and learning. We are a professional-level publisher of books and journals for K–12 educators, and we are committed to creating and providing resources that embody these qualities. Corwin's motto is "Success for All Learners."

The Exceptional Child in the Regular Classroom

An Educator's Guide

Lee Brattland Nielsen

CORWIN PRESS, INC.
A Sage Publications Company
Thousand Oaks, California

For information address:

Corwin Press, Inc.
A Sage Publications Company
2455 Teller Road
Thousand Oaks, California 91320
e-mail: order@corwin.sagepub.com

SAGE Publications Ltd.
6 Bonhill Street
London EC2A 4PU
United Kingdom

SAGE Publications India Pvt. Ltd.
M-32 Market
Greater Kailash I
New Delhi 110 048 India

Printed in the United States of America

Library of Congress Cataloging-in-Publication Data

Nielsen, Lee Brattland.
    The exceptional child in the regular classroom : an educator's
guide / Lee Brattland Nielsen.
        p.   cm.
    Includes bibliographical references.
    ISBN 0-8039-6483-8 (cloth : alk. paper). — ISBN 0-8039-6484-6
(pbk. : alk. paper)
    1. Handicapped children—Education—United States—Handbooks,
manuals, etc. 2. Mainstreaming in education—United States—
Handbooks, manuals, etc. 3. Special education—Law and
legislation—United States—Handbooks, manuals, etc.   I. Title.
    LC4031.N54   1996
    371.9'046—dc20   96-32287

This book is printed on acid-free paper.

97 98 99 00 01 10 9 8 7 6 5 4 3 2 1

Corwin Press Production Editor: S. Marlene Head
Editorial Assistant: Nicole Fountain
Typesetter: Rebecca Evans
Cover Designer: Marcia R. Finlayson

Contents

A Cautionary Note

This guidebook is not a legal document. It is intended to provide accurate information about the subject matter. It is sold with the understanding that the publisher and the author are not engaged in rendering legal or other professional services. Specifically, the recommendations contained herein are guidelines only, not legal advice, and the publisher and the author do not warrant, in any manner, their suitability for any particular usage. If legal advice or other expert assistance is required, the services of an attorney or other competent professional, with knowledge of all laws pertaining to the reader and the jurisdiction, should be sought.

Preface

As a special education resource specialist, I receive many questions regarding the various exceptionalities of children. Most questions are about children with physical or mental disabilities. I have found that there is a general lack of understanding and much misinformation about children with special needs. Unfortunately, much of this misinformation gets passed on to others. This, in turn, creates problems not only for children with disabilities, but also for others in their ultimate understanding and acceptance of such children.

While teaching at the university level, I found that most students entering my classes were also misinformed about exceptional children. As student teachers, they wanted to better understand such children, but they needed more information about specific disabilities to eradicate their misconceptions. I was motivated to write this book on children with disabilities in the hope of correcting the myths, misunderstandings, and misinformation about young students with special needs. It is only through knowledge that attitudes will be changed and educators will become less apprehensive about teaching students with disabilities.

The terminology for children with exceptional needs has been and is in constant change. The Education of the Handicapped Act, refers to "handicapped" individuals. More recently, the Individuals With Disabilities Education Act (IDEA), uses the term *disability* instead of handicap. Regardless of terminology, the challenges and issues faced by those affected are much the same.

The term *exceptional* refers to any child or youth who shows significant discrepancy between ability and achievement and who may require specialized services to meet his or her educational needs (Pierangelo & Jacoby, 1996). The focus of this book is on students with physical or mental disabilities, or both.

Teachers are often unprepared to work with students with disabilities who are placed in the regular classroom. This book provides information about the nature and characteristics of the disabilities a teacher is likely to encounter and suggests practical strategies educators can use to promote good learning experiences for all students in the regular classroom. The book is intended as a handy reference for the teacher's desk, the principal's office, or the school library.

Many books have been written about disabilities, and it can be very time consuming to research a specific exceptionality. Because most educators have huge time constraints, the major disabilities in this book are arranged alphabetically from "aphasia" to "visual processing dysfunction." This provides a quick and easy way for educators to access information about a specific disability.

The manifestation of characteristics for any given disability will vary greatly from individual to individual. So while one student may be significantly impaired by a particular condition, another with the same disability might manifest no evidence of it whatsoever, or have a degree of impairment so slight that the student has no special needs and would not be considered a student with a disability. Clearly, not everyone with a disability discussed in this book requires special education.

About the Author

Lee Brattland Nielsen received her bachelor of arts degree from the University of Minnesota. She took postgraduate studies at the University of Florida; California State University, Northridge; University of California, Berkeley; and California Lutheran University. Her California teaching credentials include a Lifetime Standard Credential, a Special Education Learning Handicapped Credential, and a Special Education Resource Specialist Credential. She also has held teaching credentials in Arizona and Florida.

She has taught for more than 25 years at the elementary, secondary, and university levels. While teaching at California Lutheran University, she taught Mainstreaming the Exceptional Student to teachers and students who were working toward their teaching credentials.

She founded and worked for 2 years as the program director of WTHS, Dade County's educational broadcasting station in Miami, Florida. During this period, she coordinated all of the educational programming.

During her teaching experience, she has worked with many children with many types of exceptionalities. As a resource specialist teacher, she is currently teaching students with learning disabilities in the Los Angeles Unified School District. She believes in a positive approach to learning, with emphasis on building self-esteem for all students.

1

What Educators Need to Know About the Law[1]

Educators and parents need to be aware that individuals with disabilities have rights and protections that are guaranteed under the law. This brief overview of the law is by no means complete. Rather, it is intended to provide a basic understanding of the laws affecting children with disabilities and their families.

Prior to the 1970s, children with disabilities had no federally guaranteed legal right to a public education. Many persons with disabilities were excluded from public education or employment. They were often confined to institutions or kept at home. In some states, such as Alaska, there were laws that provided for the exclusion from school of children who might have physical or mental incapacities. These laws were based on the belief that children with disabilities would not benefit from education and that their presence in school would have a detrimental effect on other students. We now know that these beliefs are erroneous. Laws have since been passed to give rights to and protect the rights of children with disabilities.

What the Law Provides

Although there are some differences between the laws,[2] Section 504 of the Rehabilitation Act of 1973 and Public Law 94-142 (PL 94-142), more properly known as the Education for All Handicapped Children Act (EAHCA) of 1975, subsequently renamed the Individuals with Disabilities Education Act (IDEA, 1990), mandate that all children with disabilities are entitled to a free appropriate public education in the "least restrictive environment" (LRE) in light of a student's educational needs. If a disability is so severe that even with the use of supplementary aids and services, a student's needs cannot be met

1

in the regular education classroom, a different, more restrictive, placement must be considered (Alper, Schloss, Etscheidt, & Macfarlane, 1995).

The IDEA allows for substantial sums of federal money to be allocated to state and local schools for the education of students with disabilities (but not so for Section 504).[3] Although Congress still lacks the constitutional power to *directly* regulate the public school systems, federal funding does give the government a degree of leverage in dictating educational policy. What's more, current laws require that the recipient of federal funds has an obligation not to discriminate against any adult or child who has a disability. Schools receiving this funding are required to prevent discrimination in the "school district's employment practices, access to school buildings and other facilities, and the design of new construction."

The stated purposes of the IDEA are to

assure that all children with disabilities have available to them within the time periods specified . . . a free appropriate public education which emphasizes special education and related services designed to meet their unique needs; to assure that the rights of children with disabilities and their parents or guardians are protected; to assist States and localities to provide for the education of all children with disabilities; and to assess and assure the effectiveness of efforts to educate children with disabilities. (20 U.S.C. Section 1400[c])

The IDEA provides for procedures to ensure that individuals with exceptional needs are given opportunities to interact to the "maximum extent" possible in the least restrictive environment (LRE) with children who are not disabled, unless the severity of the disability is such as to preclude such an arrangement. Thus if a child, even with support, has a disability that prevents attendance within the regular school program, a free appropriate public education for the child must be arranged that still includes special education and related services. Related services are defined as

transportation, and such developmental, corrective, and other supportive services (including speech pathology and audiology, psychological services, physical and occupational therapy, recreation, including therapeutic recreation, social work services, counseling services, including rehabilitation counseling, and medical services, except that such medical services shall be for diagnostic and evaluation purposes only) as may be required to assist a child with a disability to benefit from special education, and includes the early identification and assessment of disabling conditions in children. (20 U.S.C. 1401[a]17)

Procedural safeguards in the IDEA expanded on the safeguards already adopted by Congress as part of the Education Amendments of 1974. Moreover, state and local school districts must adopt procedures that guarantee the parents' rights. These include the right to (a) inspect all the educational records of the child, (b) obtain an independent educational evaluation of the child, (c) obtain prior notice of their rights, (d) file complaints and have them resolved by an impartial due process hearing, and (e) have a State review of the hearing held at the local level (Johnson, 1986, p. 40).

Alper et al. (1995) clearly summarize the major implications of IDEA and other federal laws which dictate how learners with disabilities are identified, assessed, placed, and taught, as follows:

1. Special education services suitable to the needs of the disabled student must be provided at no cost to the student or family.

2. Parents must receive written notification prior to the school's conducting a case study evaluation that may determine eligibility for special education services.

3. Individualized, comprehensive, and nondiscriminatory assessment must be provided for the purpose of identifying the learner's unique characteristics and needs.

4. An individualized education program (IEP) must be developed annually for students with disabilities. The IEP must contain a statement of current performance levels, annual goals, and short-term objectives, specific services to be provided, extent of participation in regular education settings, projected date for initiation of services, expected duration of services, objective criteria, and evaluation procedures.

5. An individualized family service plan (IFSP) must be provided to children with disabilities who are 3 to 5 years of age. The IFSP must contain the child's current performance levels,

family strengths and weaknesses, anticipated outcomes, necessary services, time lines for initiating and completing services, the name of the service manager, and methods for transitioning the child to appropriate services.

6. An individual transition plan (ITP) must be included with the IEPs of adolescents and young adults. The ITP is developed with the assistance of community-based vocational rehabilitation personnel. It complements the IEP by adding skills and services needed to support the transition from school to work.

7. Beyond specific educational services, students with disabilities are entitled to receive necessary related services. These include developmental, corrective, and other support services needed for the child or youth to benefit fully from the educational program. They may include transportation, counseling, medical evaluation, and physical, occupational, and recreation therapy.

8. Educational services must be provided in the least restrictive setting appropriate to the student's educational characteristics.

9. Finally, parents and guardians are entitled to due process when disputes regarding the appropriateness of the educational program occur. (pp. 8-9)

Discipline and Students With Disabilities

One of the most frequently misunderstood areas educators face when dealing with students with disabilities is discipline. Consistent with the U. S. Supreme Court's ruling in *Honig v. Doe* (1988), a school district may not unilaterally change the placement of a child with a disability for misbehavior that is a manifestation of his or her disability. At issue in Honig was a situation where a school district suspended two children with disabilities for more than 10 days, an action that violated the so called "stay-put" provision of the IDEA. This means that while a school district may discipline children with disabilities who present dangers to themselves or others, any exclusion from school for more than 10 days violates the heart of the IDEA. However, properly understood, this does not leave school officials helpless. Rather, it means that educators must first consult with parents and seek to amend a child's IEP to find a more appropriate and often more restrictive placement before removing a child with a disability who misbehaves from the classroom (*Honig v. Doe*, 484 U.S. 305 [1988]).

Recently, an amendment to IDEA has been passed which allows a school district to protect teachers and students from a dangerous student, even if the student is classified as a student with a disability. The amendment provides that a local educational agency may place a student with a disability in an alternative educational setting for up to 45 days for conduct that poses a serious danger to the safety of other students or school personnel (such as bringing a weapon to school), provided an impartial hearing is first conducted by the school agency or its designee. This amendment provides for due process hearings so that the rights of students with disabilities are protected. At the same time it enables school districts to remove violent students, even if they have disabilities, so that teachers and other students are protected (amendment to Education of the Handicapped Act, 20 U.S.C., section 1415 [e]).

The Collaborative Team

Educating students with disabilities is a shared, collaborative team effort. Depending on the student's IEP and personal needs, the team may include a special education teacher, regular education teacher, school nurse or other health care professional, school psychologist, social worker, speech-pathologist, physical therapist, occupational therapist, other professionals and consultants, building principal, and parents. The regular classroom teacher may call on one or more of these individuals for information and assistance, as needed.

A student with a disability may be placed in a regular classroom on a part-time or a full-time basis, with consultative or other assistance provided by special educators. The curriculum for a student with a disability may parallel the regular curriculum, but the regular teacher will need to modify teaching techniques and pace, course content, and evaluation methods to fit the student's special learning needs. Special educators can provide guidance to regular teachers on strategies to use with students with special needs (Alper et al., 1995).

Notes

1. The author gratefully acknowledges the assistance of Lawrence B. Trygstad, a Los Angeles attorney specializing in law relating to education, for reviewing and providing additional information for Chapter 1.

2. Section 504 and the IDEA, although similar, do differ in some important ways. For example, the IDEA covers students ages 3 to 21. Section 504 covers students and school staff of all ages, including those who may not be covered under IDEA. In addition, there is no limit to the amount of money a school district must be required to spend to provide services under the IDEA. However, Section 504 does allow a school district to discontinue services if it determines such services to be too costly.

3. There are provisions in the IDEA providing that school districts be reimbursed for a portion of their costs associated with special education, but there are no such funding provisions under Section 504.

2

How Teachers Can Create a Positive Learning Environment

Under current laws, students with disabilities should receive services in the least restrictive environment (LRE) and in regular classes, whenever feasible. This presents an increasing challenge for teachers because it is their responsibility to promote a successful learning experience for all students. The challenge is well worth the effort, however. Educators are finding that, in most cases, being in an integrated educational setting gives students with disabilities the opportunity to interact with nondisabled individuals and better prepares them for life in the real world. Students without disabilities have the opportunity to learn about the complexity and diversity of human characteristics and that shared traits and needs exceed differences (Alper, Schloss, Etscheidt, & Macfarlane, 1995).

Creating an Inclusive Environment

The educational environment has a tremendous impact on students with disabilities, as well as students without disabilities. In the process of including students with disabilities in the regular classroom, the teacher must convey positive feelings and a caring attitude toward them. The attitudes of the teacher are quickly picked up and emulated by other students. Creating a positive and comfortable environment is essential if the educational experience is to be successful and rewarding for all students.

The language one uses in referring to a student with a disability can impart negative attitudes toward the student and hinder the development of self-esteem. The teacher must avoid any language that has a negative connotation. For example, two very commonly used words are *afflicted* and *unfortunate*. *Afflicted* is very negative because it suggests the person has been singled out or cursed, and *unfortunate*

7

implies that the person with a disability is unlucky or to be pitied. Other words considered inappropriate and to be avoided include *handicapped, crippled, deformed, diseased, burdensome, spastic, incapacitated,* and *disadvantaged.*

Arranging for a student who has been in a restrictive setting to enter into a less restrictive setting requires advance preparation on the part of teachers and others involved. It must be a cooperative effort by all. A conference of the administrators and all educators who are responsible for the education of a student with a disability is essential to provide properly for the inclusion of the child in the regular classroom. The regular education teacher should also be provided with information regarding the present skills and objectives of the student along with his or her strengths and weaknesses. All education personnel who are responsible for the physical and educational needs of a student must share the responsibility for meeting those needs.

Educators need to learn about the disabling condition of a student placed in a regular classroom. The special education teacher can provide much of that information. The regular teacher should also check the student's medical and other school records. This information will guide the teacher in making appropriate modifications to the room environment and in using strategies that will best fit the educational and physical needs of the student.

The furniture and equipment of the room may need to be changed to accommodate students with disabilities. It is helpful if students with disabilities have an opportunity to become familiar with the room environment without other students being present. Prior orientation to the room will help the student to adjust and to feel comfortable and secure in the room.

Depending on the particular disability, the special education teacher can work with the regular teacher to ensure that all needed assistance devices are available for the student. These might include rubber thumbs to turn pages, pencil grips, large-type texts, or other devices that are currently available. Many professionals are available to provide assistance to the regular teacher. The teacher should check on supportive personnel services that are available. For example, psychologists, interpreters, tutors, and aides are generally available at the school site or through the district office to help the teacher. Many organizations dedicated to helping students with disabilities can also provide assistance to the teacher (see the list of public agencies at end of this book in the Resources section).

Teaching Students About Disabilities

Other students should be given accurate information, in advance, about the disability of a student who is being placed in their class. The teacher, although mindful of the need for privacy, should provide enough background information about the disability to allay any fears or misconceptions the other students may have. Students need to be made aware of the strengths of the student with disabilities as well as his or her limitations. Having regular students participate in simulated disabling activities gives them an opportunity to better understand the problems faced by the student who has a disability. Students should also be given the opportunity to learn about people with disabilities who have achieved success. Many books, films, and other audiovisual materials are available about people who have overcome their disabilities.

Positive interaction between students without disabilities and students with disabilities depends on the teacher's attitude and ability to promote a positive environment. One way of achieving this is by using cooperative learning to facilitate small-group interaction. A supportive atmosphere is created when everyone is cooperating to achieve group goals and is primarily concerned with the success of the group as a whole. When working together cooperatively, students tend to give more praise, encouragement, and support to students with disabilities. These positive experiences provide an opportunity for social and emotional growth for everyone involved.

Including Parents

Parents also have to be involved if their child is to have a rewarding experience. The teacher, before placing a child with a disability in a regular class, should invite the parents to visit the class and confer about their child. It is important to open the lines of communication. Thereafter, the regular teacher needs to communicate with the parents on a regular basis to keep them informed of the student's progress, homework and daily assignments, and any future projects that are planned. Parental involvement in the educational process and the special assistance given to the student with a disability will contribute to the student's academic success. On occasion, a teacher may offer guidance to parents on ways to help their children. For example, a teacher may tactfully encourage parents to outwardly show their affection and support for their child as he or she embarks on a new experience or achieves a new goal.

A student with a disability has the same basic needs as a student without a disability. Stressing the similarities is essential if positive interactions among all students are to be achieved. To grow emotionally and socially, students with disabilities need the support and acceptance of their peers, their teachers, and their parents.

3

Understanding the Parents of Exceptional Children

Parents of exceptional children are confronted with numerous challenges and many difficult situations that other parents never have to experience. The child with a disability—especially if it is severe—may have a profound effect on the family, and the interactions can often lead to great anxiety and frustration. Undue strain may be placed on the family structure. Relationships may either grow stronger or disintegrate because of the considerable stress of coping with the unanticipated obligations. Some parents are able to realistically and successfully adapt, whereas others are less prepared to accept the challenge of having a child with a disability in the family.

Most parents envision having a perfect child. When a disability is diagnosed, there can be any number of natural reactions, such as shock, disbelief, and even grief. But if parents demonstrate denial about the disability, they may set goals that put unrealistic pressure on the child to achieve. The parents may enroll their child in extracurricular activities such as dance lessons and karate, in which the child may not be able to perform. Often, it is only when the child is older and is with his or her peers that the disability becomes more obvious to the parents. As long as there is denial of the disabling condition, it is difficult for professionals to guide the parent. So it is important for educators to demonstrate sensitivity to the parents as well and help them establish attainable academic and social goals for the disabled child.

Parents sometimes have strong feelings of guilt and may blame themselves for having a child with a disability. Or they may blame doctors and other professionals, including teachers. It is important for teachers to not take such blame personally. The teacher needs to communicate to the parent that he or she cares, is "on their side," and wants their child to reach his or her own individual potential. It is important for the teacher to understand that parents are often just trying to find a reason for their difficult situation. Educators must keep in mind that most parents are simply doing their best to raise their child.

There is a tendency to overprotect the child with a disability more than the reality of the situation demands. Parents, as well as teachers, may feel a need to protect the child from any failure or rejection. The child is kept out of any competitive activity in which the disability may become obvious or in which there might be a chance of failure. Overprotection prevents the child from having any opportunity for problem solving and decision making, and does not foster the child's independence or social and emotional development. If the child with a disability is to grow socially and emotionally, it is necessary for parents and teachers to understand that the disabled child needs less protection rather than more. Becoming less protective allows the child to become more self-reliant and self-assured. Even though the child with a disability may not always succeed in competitive events, he or she often will feel successful in having tried if the focus is on achievement rather than on the disability. The child needs to be allowed to enter the mainstream of life whenever possible.

Unfortunately, many parents do not accept the fact that they, too, are entitled to normal lives. Even though their family life may be disrupted, there are many professionals and support groups that can help them to adjust. Parents can be guided throughout the various crises that might occur and learn how to accept the challenges of having a child with a disability. The positive environment of an intervention team of professionals and support groups can help improve their ability to confront and surmount these challenges.

Every family unit and individual is unique, with individual characteristics and abilities. A positive and caring environment is essential for the family unit. Parents and teachers need to develop self-awareness in all children by focusing on the qualities, strengths, and talents that make them unique. If given the opportunity, every child with a disability can contribute to the family experience.

4 Disabilities and Health Disorders: Strategies for Educators

It is only through knowledge that the many commonly held misconceptions about disabilities will be dispelled and a better understanding of the needs of students with disabilities will be gained. The background and characteristics of specific disabilities are discussed in this chapter. The specific disabilities are arranged alphabetically to provide quick and easy reference.

Many of the characteristics for one type of disability can also be found under other types of disabilities. Given the overlap among different disabilities, many of the suggestions in this chapter for teaching a student with a particular disability can be successfully applied to one with another disability.

Educators have always used many different teaching strategies to meet the needs of their students. When students with disabilities are in the regular classroom, additional strategies are needed. Strategies for educators are discussed under each specific disability.

Aphasia

Definition

Aphasia is the total or partial loss of the ability to make sense of spoken or written language, irrespective of intelligence.

Background

Aphasia is not a disease but rather a symptom of brain damage. It can be the result of a stroke, brain tumor, infection, or head injury. Physicians often mistakenly consider aphasia to be the result of confusion or mental disturbance. As such, it is difficult to determine how many people have aphasia as it may not be reported and the brain injury is not detected.

There are different types of aphasia. One type, called *receptive aphasia*, causes problems in comprehension. Even though the speech of the aphasic may be fluent, his or her impaired comprehension distorts what is heard or what is seen in print. The aphasic hears the voice or sees the print but is unable to make sense of the words. This type of aphasia is also referred to as *Wernicke's aphasia*, because damage to the Wernicke's area in the brain causes the problem.

Another type of aphasia is *global aphasia*, in which there is total or almost total inability to speak, write, or understand the written word. All language functions, including expression and comprehension, are lost. Global aphasia is due to extensive damage to the language areas of the brain.

Nominal aphasia, also referred to as *anomic aphasia* or *amnesic aphasia*, is a milder form of aphasia, which manifests when someone has trouble correctly naming objects, people, places, or events. According to the American Medical Association, it may be caused by a "generalized cerebral dysfunction or damage to specific language areas."

Expressive aphasia, also called *Broca's aphasia*, causes difficulty in language expression. A person with this type of aphasia is able to use only a few meaningful words. The speech is not only nonfluent but generally very slow and deliberate. Damage to the Broca's area of the brain causes this type of aphasia.

If a brain injury occurs in a child whose speech and language have just begun to develop, he or she may have what is called *acquired aphasia*, or the loss of language. This can occur when blood flow to the brain is blocked during surgery or the child has a severe head trauma or brain infection. A child who has an acquired aphasic condition is better able to recover than an adult who has acquired it. Fortunately, the neurons in a child's brain seem to be capable of compensating for the injury, and the brain will continue to reorganize itself until adolescence.

Because of the variables, it is impossible to obtain accurate statistics as to how many people suffer from aphasia. However, according to the U.S. Department of Health and Human Services, 20% of those who have had a stroke develop aphasia. Some researchers estimate that there may be 1 million people in the United States who are aphasic, but that number is increasing because the number of people who now survive strokes is also increasing, and many of those survivors develop aphasia.

The American Medical Association states that there is less chance of complete recovery in severe cases of aphasia, but after a stroke or head injury some recovery from aphasia can be expected.

Characteristics

The symptoms of aphasia vary greatly, depending on the severity of language loss. In addition to the effects of aphasia, many of the following characteristics have been experienced by some aphasics:

- Muscle weakness
- Paralysis on one side of the body
- Frequent headaches
- Seizures
- Loss of peripheral vision
- Hearing impairments
- Articulation problems
- Inability to produce voice
- Making incomplete sentences
- Syntax errors
- Inability to understand symbolic meanings
- Short attention span
- Memory difficulties
- Shifting moods
- Tears and laughter for no apparent reason
- Loss of personal habits
- Compulsive neatness and orderliness
- Feelings of helplessness
- Lethargy
- Fatigue
- Depression

- Feelings of unworthiness
- Memory loss
- Inability to perform simple tasks

Strategies for Educators

Because most aphasics are taught in special classes, the regular classroom may have students who are only mildly aphasic. In this case, the teacher needs to bear in mind that the receptive aphasic will not perceive the complete stimuli. The teacher will have to encourage the student to use other cues, such as sight and the olfactory, tactile, and kinesthetic senses, to help him or her formulate meaning from the spoken expression or visual symbol. In some cases, the student with aphasia may be unable to distinguish an item by sight, but if other senses are used, the item can be identified. The teacher must make allowances for the deficit and for the communication needs of the aphasic. As with many disabilities, the teacher needs to use a multisensory approach.

The physiological and psychological effects of aphasia can be devastating to a child. It is degrading to the student with aphasia if the teacher treats him or her as being mentally incompetent. Self-esteem suffers and recovery is slowed. The frustration and annoyance experienced by the aphasic cannot be underestimated. When the ability to communicate is gone, a person feels helpless and isolated.

It is crucial that the teacher facilitate the socialization process for a student with aphasia by providing opportunities for him or her to join other students in cooperative classroom activities. A dependable "buddy" can help in the socialization process of the student. Appropriate extracurricular activities can aid the student in the communication process. All students, including the student with aphasia, learn best when the communication process is fun.

Results of medical and therapy intervention cannot be accurately predicted, but many aphasics do regain their capacity for language. The teacher can expect these students to be in the regular classroom. Although some aphasics may never regain their language skills, they will still be able to participate in family activities and enjoy social gatherings.

Attention Deficit Disorder and
Attention Deficit Hyperactivity Disorder

Definition

Attention deficit disorder (ADD) and attention deficit hyperactivity disorder (ADHD) are developmental disabilities that result in inattentiveness, impulsiveness, and, in some cases, hyperactivity.

Background

Previously, attention deficit disorder was referred to in two ways: as ADD with hyperactivity and as ADD without hyperactivity. In 1987, the acronym for ADD with hyperactivity was changed to ADHD. Eighty percent of people with an attention deficit disorder are hyperactive (University of California Office of the President, 1996). This high percentage reflects the predominance of hyperactivity as a characteristic for the vast majority of persons with this disorder. However, many children who are not hyperactive still have ADD.

In some cases, ADHD is caused by a chemical imbalance in which certain neurotransmitters, the chemicals that regulate the efficiency with which the brain controls behavior, are deficient. Other research implicates fetal exposure to lead, alcohol, or cigarette smoke. A 1990 study by Alan Zametkin et al. at the National Institute of Mental Health showed that the rate at which the brain utilizes glucose is slower in persons with ADHD than in the rest of the population. Although the exact cause of ADHD is unknown at this time, the current consensus is that ADHD is a neurological medical problem and not the result of poor parenting or diet.

Other research has indicated that ADHD is genetically transmitted. Russell Barkley of the University of Massachusetts states that almost half of children with ADHD have a parent who also has the disorder and that one third have siblings with ADHD (University of California Office of the President, 1996).

It is estimated that 3% to 5% of children have ADHD. It is also estimated that between 50% and 65% of the children affected with ADHD will continue to have the symptoms of the disorder as adolescents and adults. More than 2 million adults are reported to suffer from ADHD.

P. M. Wender, professor of psychiatry at the University of Utah School of Medicine, states that children suffering from ADHD "appear in accident [emergency] rooms at five times the expected rate" (quoted in Wolkenberg, 1987). Studies show that 50% of adolescents with ADHD get into trouble with the law. According to Lily Hechtman, a Canadian psychiatrist, ADHD alone is not responsible for their antisocial behavior but "any hardship is a risk factor whether it be from a lower socioeconomic background, IQ . . . ADD is just one more" (Wolkenberg, 1987). Since 1902, a great deal of medical literature describing ADHD has been published, and children have been treated for this disorder for the past five decades. However, it is only recently that standardized criteria have been used in the diagnosis of ADHD. According to the American Psychiatric Association's *Diagnostic and Statistical Manual of Mental Disorders* (1994, pp. 83-85), there are 14 behaviors associated with a person who has ADHD that indicate the need for further evaluation. These behaviors are listed below under Characteristics. If eight or more of the behaviors are present before the age of 7 and have continued for at least 6 months, the child is considered to have an attention deficit hyperactivity disorder. Identifying these symptoms prior to school age is essential in order to rule out the possibility that the behaviors are just a reaction to school adjustment.

It is important to understand that there is no simple test, such as a blood test or urinalysis, to determine if a person has ADHD. Accurate diagnosis is not only complicated but requires assessment by well-trained professionals, such as a developmental pediatrician, child psychologist, child psychiatrist, or pediatric neurologist. ADHD is a disability that requires proper diagnosis and treatment to prevent long-term, serious complications.

Effective treatment for individuals with ADHD generally requires three basic components: medication, behavior management, and appropriate educational programs.

Medication, although controversial, has been effective with many children diagnosed with ADHD. Stimulants are the most widely prescribed type of medication. These drugs stimulate the brain's neurotransmitters to enable it to better regulate attention, impulsiveness, and motor behavior. For children who are unable to take stimulant medications, antidepressant medication is prescribed.

According to pediatricians Robin L. Hansen and Penelope G. Krener (University of California Office of the President, 1996) at the University of California, Davis, medication is overprescribed for children with ADHD. The decision to use medication should be made only after a very thorough evaluation by the physician and consultation with the parent.

Since 1990, the number of people who have been diagnosed as having ADHD has doubled to 2 million. Some researchers believe that children with "presumed attention or behavior problems" may not always have an attention deficit hyperactivity disorder. Before a diagnosis of ADHD is made, a comprehensive evaluation is essential (University of California Office of the President, 1996).

Educators often have unrealistic expectations about what constitutes normal behavior in children. For example, it is not realistic to expect children to remain quiet and restricted for 4 to 6 hours. Such expectations go against the normal developmental behavior of children.

There is also the possibility that TV may be contributing to a decrease in both the attention span and the ability to concentrate in all children. Society needs to take a closer look at the effects of TV on children.

Characteristics

The diagnostic criteria for those who suffer from ADHD, as listed in the American Psychiatric Association's *Diagnostic and Statistical Manual of Mental Disorders* (1994), are as follows:

- Often fidgets with hands or feet, or squirms in seat (in adolescents, may be limited to subjective feelings of restlessness)
- Has difficulty remaining seated when required to do so
- Is easily distracted by extraneous stimuli
- Has difficulty awaiting turn in games or group situations
- Often blurts out answers to questions before they have been completed
- Has difficulty following through on instructions from others (not due to oppositional behavior or failure to comprehend directions); doesn't complete chores
- Has difficulty sustaining attention in tasks and play activities

- Often shifts from one uncompleted activity to another
- Has difficulty playing quietly
- Often talks excessively
- Often interrupts or intrudes on others (butts into other children's games)
- Often does not seem to listen to what is being said to him or her
- Often loses things necessary for tasks or activities at school or at home (toys, pencils, books, assignments)
- Often engages in physically dangerous activities (runs into street without looking) without considering possible consequences (not for the purpose of thrill-seeking)
- Behaviors begin before the age of 7 (pp. 83-85)

Strategies for Educators

Developing the student with ADHD's sense of competency and responsibility is necessary. The teacher needs to identify the student's weaknesses and strengths, and to provide opportunities to build on the strengths in order to help such individuals develop a better self-image. Equally important is the need to develop realistic expectations for the child with ADHD.

Because most children with ADHD suffer from low self-esteem and are mildly depressed, understanding, encouragement, and praise are essential. These children are continually bombarded with negative feedback and punishment. It is essential that all students who may have ADHD are properly diagnosed so that corrective measures can be taken.

It can be difficult for students with ADHD to adapt to the classroom regime because of their low self-esteem, outbursts of temper, and low frustration tolerance. Some, but not all, may have learning disabilities that add to their frustration.

Likewise, it can be difficult for teachers who have students with ADHD in the regular classroom. The inattention, impulsiveness, and hyperactivity of a student with ADHD are not only disruptive but also tend to affect the behaviors and attitudes of the other students in the class. It is important for the teacher to be knowledgeable about the disorder in order to meet the educational needs of all students and make the appropriate classroom modifications.

A student with ADHD responds to a well-structured environment. The student with ADHD is often easily distracted, so any stimuli that may distract the student should be avoided. For instance, whenever possible, he or she should not be seated near a window or door or any unusually high-traffic areas. Heaters, air conditioners, fans, and other equipment also divert the attention of the student. Seating the student in a study carrel, however, may also produce a negative effect, because the student may create unruly distractions by tapping the feet, hands, pencil, book, or notebook. It is best that he or she remain as part of the class and possibly be seated between other peers who are respected by the class. If the student is seated near the teacher's desk, his or her back should be toward the rest of the class so there will be fewer distracting influences.

The teacher should place a high priority on orderliness and neatness for the student with ADHD. Depending on the student's age, the teacher may need to teach organization skills. A student with ADHD generally has a very cluttered desk, so teachers should help organize his or her materials. The student with ADHD should not only straighten those belongings daily but always clear out any unnecessary material.

Depending on the age of the student, one method of organizing different subject matter is to use color coding. Colored tapes that denote different subjects can be used inside the desk as an organizational tool. The student's notebook can also be maintained in the same manner; for example, a blue divider might be used for math, green for homework, yellow for language, and other colors for different subjects.

Methods used for all students to maintain their attention are equally effective for the student with ADHD. Teachers should always give clear and concise directions to the student with ADHD. Complex directions only confuse the student and prevent him or her from accomplishing the task. When giving oral directions, it is best to give one direction at a time and to maintain eye contact with the student. Because the student with ADHD often goes from one task to another, and completes neither, give only one assignment at a time. Whenever possible, the directions should be both oral and written. Because of the heightened distractibility of a student with ADHD, it is often helpful to restate the directions to refocus his or her attention. As often as possible, the student should be actively involved in paraphrasing and repeating the directions back to the teacher.

Secondary students with ADHD will benefit by copying their weekly assignments on a spreadsheet and having the teacher initial each one. This makes it possible for all of the student's teachers to make certain that the assignments are accurate. Teachers should make duplicate texts and a copy of the spreadsheet available to the parent.

There is a need for the teacher to stress quality rather than quantity. By stressing quality, the student will be less pressured by time and be able to accomplish the task to the best of his or her ability. The teacher thereby relieves the student with ADHD of much of the excessive pressure to complete the work that he or she may feel.

The student with ADHD usually acts on impulse, blurting out answers in a class or becoming physically abusive, with little regard for the consequences of such actions. A behavioral management system can be very successful in controlling this impulsive behavior if the student clearly understands what is expected. The main principle of behavior management is to increase the student's appropriate behavior and to decrease inappropriate behavior through the use of consequences. Rewarding appropriate behavior will generally increase it. Some psychologists believe that ignoring inappropriate behavior helps to decrease its frequency.

Making a contract with the student may motivate him or her to gradually bring the undesired behavior under control. Providing the student with a checklist of desired behavioral outcomes will give the student a feeling of individual control, develop his or her awareness of the problem, and help improve his or her self-management. The daily checklist for the specified behavior should be positively worded, using terms such as *fair, good,* and *better.* The student can then determine his or her growth in achieving the established goal. If a token economy system is used, rewards valued by the student for achieving certain targeted goals should be prearranged. As always, give positive reinforcement for various levels of achievement of the targeted goals.

Much of the inappropriate behavior of students with ADHD evokes negative responses from others, which may have a detrimental effect on their social and emotional growth. Praise and a behavior management program that promotes self-discipline are necessary to create an atmosphere in which students with ADHD feel comfortable and engage in learning activities.

Auditory Processing Dysfunction

Definition

H. R. Myklebust, a psychologist and educator recognized for his distinguished service to exceptional children, defines *auditory processing* as the ability to "structure the auditory world and select those sounds that are immediately pertinent to adjustment" (Chalfant & Scheffelin, 1969, p. 9). The inability to accurately process receptive or expressive auditory stimuli is considered to be a dysfunction. The term has also been used to describe many behavioral responses to auditory stimuli.

Background

The auditory channel is one of the most important avenues through which we receive information about our environment. Even though the hearing acuity is within the normal range, someone with an auditory processing disorder has difficulty processing and obtaining meaning from auditory stimuli.

Many theorists attempt to attribute the localization of sensory perception to an isolated area of the brain. There is some evidence that suggests that the primary receiving strip for auditory stimuli is located in the Sylvian margin of the temporal lobe. It may be here that the complex forms of auditory analysis and integration occur. This region may be largely responsible for the systematic deciphering of sound signals necessary for the perception of speech. Research concerning the function of the secondary divisions of the auditory cortex is less clear.

Children who have difficulty processing auditory stimuli may have trouble identifying the source of sounds or understanding the meaning of environmental sounds. It is difficult for them to differentiate between significant and insignificant stimuli. There is also evidence that people with an auditory processing deficit have difficulty reproducing pitch, rhythm, and melody.

Characteristics

Children with an auditory processing dysfunction often have a deficit in discrimination skills. They have difficulty both hearing vowel sounds or the soft consonant sounds in spoken words and understanding subtle differences in sounds. Words and phrases are misidentified; for example, "blue" might be mistaken for "ball," or "ball" for "bell." If children are unable to recognize auditory differences and similarities, they will have difficulty in acquiring and understanding the spoken language.

Children with auditory discrimination deficit have difficulty not only in determining if the language sounds of two words are the same or different but also whether the initial, medial, or final sounds of two words are the same or different. This deficit also carries over to the discrimination of blended sounds.

The analysis and synthesis of a series of speech sounds is essential to learning the phonemic structure of language. A deficit that affects the auditory memory, speech, and reading ability of the individual has far-reaching implications in education. Because many students improve these skills until their eighth year (but they never completely close the gap), the chronological age of the individual should always be taken into consideration in determining the severity of the disability.

A common characteristic of a person with an auditory processing dysfunction, and one that is often mistaken for inattention, is the inability to isolate a sound from background sounds. This creates a problem when there is an attempt to retrieve the needed auditory impression from memory. The auditory sequential memory is affected and it is difficult for the individual to remember oral directions or the sequence of events. The individual's inattention, due to the auditory sequential memory deficit, makes it extremely difficult to attend to auditory stimuli and many environmental and speech sounds. The implications for a person with an auditory processing problem are clear.

Strategies for Educators

Some students may have an auditory processing dysfunction that has not been identified. Those who have been identified as having an auditory processing dysfunction are helped in special education classes and also by being included in regular classes.

Students who have an auditory processing dysfunction learn best when the teacher presents information in a visual mode, so teachers should seat students where eye contact can easily be made. Remember: A student with an auditory processing dysfunction has

difficulty following the verbal directions and explanations, so ver
instructions should be interrelated with visual stimuli and dem-
onstrations. Students with this disability should be asked to repeat
back directions to be sure they understand.

The teacher is obligated to provide instruction that is meaningful
for students who may have an auditory processing dysfunction. It is
inappropriate for the teacher to use a phonetically based instruction
in reading for students with auditory processing dysfunctions. The
use of sight words and the configuration of words is more appropriate when teaching students to read. Teachers should use visual stimuli, such as pictures, whenever possible. Students will enjoy reading
descriptive material because of the visualization required. The
teacher can expect excellent responses when asking students to re-
late details that involve visual imagery, and students should be encouraged to apply their visualization skills to creative writing. As
with all students, positive feedback will encourage the students with
auditory processing dysfunctions to continue with their writing
endeavors.

Autism

Definition

There are various definitions of *autism*. One definition is that
autism is a neurological or brain disorder characterized by a decrease in communication and social interactions. *The New Lexicon
Webster's Encyclopedic Dictionary of the English Language* (1991) defines autism as a psychiatric disorder in which the person withdraws
into himself or herself, is unresponsive to external events, and shows
indifference to individuals and external happenings. The Los Angeles
chapter of the Autism Society of America defines autism as a lifelong
developmental disability with disturbances in "physical, social, and
language skills" (Gillingham, 1995, p. 8).

Background

Although autism has had a long past, it was not until 1943 that
Leo Kanner, a child psychiatrist at Johns Hopkins University Medical School, named this developmental disorder *autism*. He borrowed
the name from Eugene Bleuler, a Swiss psychiatrist, who used the

term in 1911 to describe the active withdrawal from social inter-actions of his schizophrenic patients.

From the 1940s through the 1960s, it was generally believed that people with autism had a conscious desire to withdraw from any social interaction. However, today it is understood that the with-drawal is not a conscious desire but rather the result of neurological and biochemical alterations in the brain.

The exact cause of autism is unknown. At one point, it was thought that a lack of warmth from parents caused the disorder. This has been proven to be untrue. Autism is not caused by psychological factors. All evidence indicates that autism has a biological origin resulting in a metabolic dysfunction of the brain. Because about one quarter of autistic children have signs of a neurological disorder, it is possible that they have a degree of brain damage. Bernard Rimland, the foun-der of the National Society for Autistic Children, director of the Autism Research Institute in San Diego, and an early advocate in the use of behavior modification, believes that there is a neurological cause of autism that involves a possible dysfunction of the brain stem reticular formation. The reticular formation is the web of nerve cells in the brain stem that is involved in perception. A perceptual malfunction may be the result of impaired reticular functioning.

Autism occurs in all socioeconomic classes, although it seems to be more prevalent in the higher socioeconomic classes. However, this may be attributed to the fact that better educated families are more apt to recognize autistic-like behavior in their child and to seek help. Because of the varied definitions of autism, there are different estimates as to its incidence, but according to the American Medical Association, autism occurs in about two to four of every 10,000 births. It is three times more common in boys than in girls. Autism is rarely found to affect more than one child in a family.

A child with autism appears normal for the first few months of life. The symptoms of autism emerge as the child develops and the deficit progresses. According to the American Medical Association, autism usually becomes evident by the age of 30 months. The child fails to develop language skills appropriate for his or her age. Indi-cations that a child is autistic become apparent as he or she becomes unresponsive to the parents or any stimuli. The child may resist cud-dling by the parents and, when picked up, may scream until he or she is put down. This may occur even if the child is not hurt or tired.

The intellect of children with autism is generally well below normal, with 70% being mentally retarded. Thirty percent of people with autism have average or above-average intellect. As in the general population, there is a wide variance in intellectual ability. In addition, there is a basic difference between the person with autism who is also mentally retarded and the person who is mentally retarded. In the mentally retarded, there is a generalized developmental delay. In the autistic, delays in development vary over the person's life span.

The impairment of language development in children with autism has always presented a challenge to parents and educators. In the early 1960s, Rosalind Oppenheim, founder of the Illinois School for Autistic Children, attempted to meet this challenge. She discovered that her son was able to compose sentences on a typewriter as she touched his hand. This method was originally referred to as a "talking typewriter" and now is known as "facilitated communication."

In facilitated communication, another person "holds and guides the subject's hand over the keyboard" (Shapiro, 1992, p. 63), allowing the subject to express thoughts by way of the keyboard. To date, facilitated communication has not been objectively or scientifically verified by independent researchers, and many believe it is nothing more than the facilitator expressing his or her own thoughts and feelings. Still, there are parents who are very enthusiastic about facilitated communication and report that they have had excellent results using the method.

In 1989, a Syracuse University special education professor, Douglas Biklen, observed facilitated communication as it was being used by Rosemary Crossley, a teacher in Australia (Shapiro, 1992). He was impressed with the results and returned to the United States to teach the method of facilitated communication. Recently, he opened a Facilitated Communication Center in Syracuse. Biklin has thus far refused to have any independent scientific studies done as to verify the claimed success of the method.

The controversy continues over whether the facilitator or the child with autism is doing the communicating on the typewriter or computer. An article by Paul Heinrichs (1991) in a Melbourne newspaper, *The Sunday Age*, quoted Robert Cummins, a senior lecturer at Victoria College, as saying, "It's time to call a halt to the charade. . . . [facilitated communication is] an apparent cult of deception or illusion." The American Psychological Association states that facilitated communication is not a proven communication procedure. At present, no scientific studies exist that confirm the validity of the procedure.

Erroneous beliefs about autism often have led to the removal of the child with autism from the home. This has changed as the result of increasing advances in research about and our understanding of autism. New and innovative techniques are now used in the treatment of children with autism. In addition, greater help is available for parents.

Characteristics

Not all autistic people manifest every characteristic, but the following are typical characteristics of autism:

- Difficulty relating to people, objects, and events
- Using toys and objects in an unconventional manner
- Lack of interaction with other children
- Appearing to be unaware of others
- Treating others as inanimate objects
- Avoiding eye contact
- Inability to accept affection
- Dislike of being touched
- Insistence that the environment and routine remain unchanged
- Compulsive and ritualistic behaviors
- Self-stimulatory behavior
- Self-injurious behavior, such as head banging
- Hyper- or hyposensitivity to various sensory stimuli
- Tantrums, often for no apparent reason
- Violent behavior toward others
- Severely impaired verbal and nonverbal communication skills
- Inability to communicate with words or gestures
- Nonspeech vocalizations
- Repetition of other's words (echolalia)
- Repetition of something heard earlier (delayed echolalia)
- Preoccupation with hands

The child may appear to be deaf yet be able to hear soft words spoken in the distance. This denial of hearing is a very common characteristic. Parents and others working with the child should never take the child's denial and behaviors personally.

It should be noted that any one or more of the characteristics of autism may occur in children with other disabilities. In these cases, the phrase *autistic-like behavior* is used.

Strategies for Educators

There is skepticism about placing a student with autism in a regular classroom setting. However, in some small school districts, there have been no separate facilities to accommodate the few children with autism who enrolled in the school. The children with autism had to be enrolled in the regular classroom. They were observed to do better than the autistic children in other districts who were enrolled in a tailored classroom. The theory is that by separating children with autism from a normal environment, their problems only intensify.

Emphasis in education should be on helping children who are autistic learn ways to communicate and on structuring their environment so that it is consistent and predictable. The teacher can help by providing calendars, photos, or pictures of activities or events before they occur.

Effective teaching includes attention to behavior plans, positive behavior management, and clear expectations and rules. The student with autism needs to know the expectations a teacher has and the consequence of failing to meet those expectations.

Many students with autism are visual learners. The use of concrete, tangible visual aids, such as pictures or charts, is essential. Much of the material used for students with learning disabilities is appropriate for students who are autistic.

Some students with autism are skillful in drawing, music, and mathematics, and they often have normal or advanced competency in these areas. The teacher should encourage such students' talents, provide additional learning opportunities in these areas, and always provide positive reinforcement.

Making generalizations is very difficult for autistic students. They need to practice skills that are functional for real-life situations. For example, it is best to use real foods in the study of nutrition.

When teaching money skills, the teacher should use real money rather than play money. Whenever possible, the students should be taken to real places when learning about and practicing acceptable public behavior. Class field trips provide excellent concrete learning experiences for the student who is autistic.

It is advantageous for the regular class students to learn about the difficulties a child with autism has to overcome. Insights into the problems can be gained through stories and books written by parents who have autistic children. Well-known authors who have written about their autistic sons include Sylvester Stallone, actor; William Christopher, actor; Beverly Sills, singer; Myron Cope, sportscaster; and Charles A. Amenta III, writer. Those who have become successful despite their own autism include Sean Barron, writer; Thomas A. McKeen, writer; Moe Norman, Canadian professional golfer; Temple Grandin, an assistant professor of animal sciences at Colorado State University; and Donna Williams, writer. Grandin wrote *Emergence: Labelled Autistic* (1986) and *Thinking in Pictures* (1995), two books that give the reader insights into the mind and emotions of a person with autism. Grandin received her Ph.D. in animal science from the University of Illinois. She has designed one third of all livestock handling facilities in the United States; these types of facilities are being used throughout the world. Williams graduated from college and has written two autobiographies, *Nobody Nowhere* (1992) and *Somebody Somewhere* (1994), that give the reader an understanding of the struggles of a person with autism.

Educators should be aware of the many problems faced by parents of autistic children. These parents may need advice on seeking professional help. There are many organizations and support groups that will offer help and guidance to them. (Check your local telephone directory for the chapter of the Autism Society of America nearest you.)

Early diagnosis and educational evaluation of autism are very important, although help given at any age can make a significant difference. Some people with autism will need supervision throughout their lives. According to Bernard Rimland, director of the Autism Research Institute, although autism is a lifelong condition, "a small percentage do recover to the point that they can live independently, and, in several cases, become world-famous" (personal communication, April 12, 1996).

Cerebral Palsy

Definition

Cerebral palsy is a group of disorders characterized by nerve and muscle dysfunctions that affect body movement and muscle control. *Cerebral* refers to the brain and *palsy* refers to a disorder of movement or posture.

Background

In 1862, William Little summarized 20 years of research by stating that spasticity and deformity associated with cerebral palsy were due to cerebral hemorrhage resulting from trauma during the birth process. During the latter part of the 19th century, Sigmund Freud made a distinction between congenital and acquired palsy and placed greater emphasis on "intra-uterine development" than on actual birth trauma.

Even though researchers in Europe had shown great interest in cerebral palsy, little interest was shown in the United States during the first quarter of this century. As stated by Leon Sternfeld (1988) in a discussion on the history of research in cerebral palsy, it was not until after World War II that interest in cerebral palsy was rekindled. The American Academy for Cerebral Palsy was organized in 1947 and the United Cerebral Palsy Association, a national organization, was formed in 1949–1950. Congress authorized the establishment of the National Institute of Neurologic and Communicative Disorders, which is very instrumental in providing information to the public.

Between 500,000 and 700,000 Americans have some degree of cerebral palsy. Each year about 5,000 infants and babies are diagnosed as having cerebral palsy, and an estimated 1,200 to 1,500 preschool-age children acquire cerebral palsy.

According to the American Medical Association, 90% of the cases of cerebral palsy occur before or at birth. Any damage to the brain may result in cerebral palsy. The causes include infection of the mother with German measles or other viral diseases during pregnancy; premature delivery; and lack of oxygen supply to the infant due to premature separation of the placenta, an awkward birth position, labor that goes on too long or is too abrupt, or interference with the umbilical cord. Cerebral palsy may be associated with Rh or ABO blood type incompatibility between parents, microorganisms that attack the newborn's central nervous system, or the lack of good prenatal care.

It is also possible to have an acquired type of cerebral palsy resulting from head injuries. Motor vehicle accidents, falls, or child abuse that results in a head injury to the child can also cause cerebral palsy. Brain infection can be another cause.

There are three main types of cerebral palsy: *spastic cerebral palsy, athetoid cerebral palsy,* and *ataxic cerebral palsy.*

Spastic cerebral palsy is the most common form. In this type of cerebral palsy, the muscles are tense, contracted, and resistant to movement. The lower legs may turn in and cross at the ankles, and movement is slow. Sometimes the leg muscles are so contracted that the child's heels do not touch the floor and the child has to walk on tiptoe. The use of physical therapy, plaster casts, and/or orthopedic surgery may help alleviate the problems.

Athetoid cerebral palsy is characterized by involuntary movements of parts of the body that are affected, such as facial grimaces, hand twisting, or tonguing and drooling. The person's body may make jerking and flailing motions. Because of these characteristics, many who have athetoid cerebral palsy are mistakenly considered to be mentally or emotionally unstable.

Ataxic cerebral palsy involves disturbances such as a lack of balance, coordination, and depth perception. With ataxic cerebral palsy, there may be swaying when standing and difficulty in maintaining balance. Persons with this type of cerebral palsy may walk with their feet wide apart in order to avoid falling. This disability, as with other disabilities, varies from mild to severe and, in some cases of ataxic cerebral palsy, there may be a complete loss of mobility.

If several motor centers are affected, the symptoms of cerebral palsy may be mixed, with a combination of the characteristics of all three main types of cerebral palsy affecting the same or different parts of the body. Although individuals may have a combination of these types of cerebral palsy, it is believed that most affected children have either spastic or athetoid cerebral palsy.

According to the American Medical Association, about 75% of individuals with cerebral palsy have mental retardation, with an IQ below 70. The exceptions are important, because some people who have spastic or athetoid cerebral palsy are highly intelligent.

Cerebral palsy is not contagious and is only rarely associated with a hereditary condition. Because brain damage does not worsen over time, cerebral palsy is nonprogressive and is not a primary cause of a person's death. Fortunately, researchers are now finding ways to prevent and treat cases of cerebral palsy.

Characteristics

Depending on which part of the brain has been damaged and the degree of involvement of the central nervous system, one or more of the following may occur:

- Spasms
- Muscle tone problems
- Involuntary movements
- Disturbances in gait and mobility
- Seizures
- Abnormal sensation and perception
- Impairment of sight
- Impairment of hearing
- Impairment of speech
- Mental retardation

All of these characteristics are not necessarily present in all cases of cerebral palsy. In some instances, there may be only a slight disturbance that is unnoticed by the teacher or students.

Strategies for Educators

As with other disabilities, the teacher needs to provide students with information regarding cerebral palsy. Many students are still under the impression that cerebral palsy is contagious. It is important for the teacher to stress the fact that cerebral palsy is neither contagious nor is it a disease. With knowledge, the students will forgo any previous misconceptions they may have held about cerebral palsy.

The teacher should select another student who will be a "buddy" to the student with cerebral palsy. The help given by the buddy should be such that the independence of the student with cerebral palsy is not jeopardized. The choice of the buddy is important. The teacher should select a dependable student who will not only help but, most important, provide companionship as well.

The teacher should have assistance equipment used by students with cerebral palsy available. These devices might include adapted typewriters, pencil holders, book holders, and page holders, as well as wheelchairs and helmets. Under the teacher's guidance and supervision, students should be given the opportunity to use these devices. Students who have used the various types of devices will better appreciate some of the difficulties faced by students who are dependent on specialized equipment for their daily existence.

In some cases, it may be necessary to schedule restroom breaks for the student, with a paraprofessional to provide assistance. It is best to schedule the break time to occur before the regular class breaks to allow the student with cerebral palsy additional time.

The handling of students with cerebral palsy, such as moving them from one position to another, depends on the nature of the various characteristics displayed by each individual. If he or she has another coexisting disability, suggestions for strategies to use with the student can be found in this book under that disability. The one thing that needs to remain constant is that the teacher be thoughtful and sensitive to the needs of the student.

Many advances have taken place in the last 15 years that have had an enormous positive effect on the long-term well-being of children born with cerebral palsy. Technological innovations have made it possible for many persons with cerebral palsy to be employed and have lives as near to normal as possible.

Down Syndrome

Definition

Down syndrome is a chromosomal disorder resulting in a delay in physical, intellectual, and language development. It is the most commonly recognizable chromosomal disorder associated with mental retardation. People with Down syndrome have a characteristic physical appearance.

Background

In 1959, researchers discovered that those who have Down syndrome also have an extra chromosome. Instead of 46 chromosomes, a person with Down syndrome has 47. This causes changes in the development of the body and the brain. In most cases, the extra chromosome is number 21. The disorder is also called Trisomy 21 (National Down Syndrome Society, 1993a, 1993b).

Because of the distinctive physical features associated with Down syndrome, it is usually recognized at birth. The diagnosis is confirmed by taking a blood sample and counting the chromosomes in the white blood cells. Through advances in molecular biology, the extra chromosome 21 that causes this developmental disorder was discovered by Jerome Lejeune in 1959. Chromosome 21 has only 1,000 to 1,500 of the 100,000 human genes. However, researchers have linked these genes to diseases such as cancer, leukemia, congenital heart defects, and vision problems.

Of all the chromosome-related disorders, Down syndrome is the most prevalent. It is estimated that one in every 800 to 1,100 live births results in a child with Down syndrome. In the United States, approximately 5,000 children annually are born with Down syndrome. Research has indicated that significantly more males than females are born with this chromosomal disorder.

Either the father or the mother may carry the extra chromosome. However, in 70% to 80% of the cases, the extra chromosome originates with the mother.

Eighty percent of children with Down syndrome are born to women under 35 years of age, but the rate of incidence is higher for women over age 35. At age 40, the chance of having a baby with Down syndrome is 1 in 110 births. At age 45, the risk increases to approximately 1 in 35 births. Women who have Down syndrome can and do have children, and there is a 50% chance that their children will also have Down syndrome.

The mortality rate of children with Down syndrome is down. Around 1910, the life expectancy for children with Down syndrome was 9 years. The National Down Syndrome Society (1993a, 1993b) states that with the recent advances in medical treatment, around 80% of adults with Down syndrome now reach age 55 and beyond. In addition, many individuals now postpone having a family until later in life, when the incidence rate of Down syndrome is higher. Thus the number of Down syndrome cases is expected to increase and possibly double in the next 10 years (National Down Syndrome Society, 1993a, 1993b).

Scientific and medical research on Down syndrome is gaining momentum, and it is hoped that eventually Down syndrome can be prevented.

Characteristics

Individuals with Down syndrome are usually smaller than their non–Down syndrome peers. Not only is their physical development slower but their intellectual development is also delayed. According to the American Medical Association, the IQ of a child with Down syndrome may range anywhere from 30 to 80, although in some cases it may be as high as 120. The mental retardation of individuals with Down syndrome falls within the range of minimal to severe, with many who are mildly to moderately disabled.

Approximately one third of babies born with Down syndrome have heart defects, most of which can now be surgically corrected. Adults with Down syndrome are prone to atherosclerosis, which can lead to heart disease.

Gastrointestinal problems are also common. Many who have Down syndrome have a higher-than-average incidence of a narrowing at some point in the intestines.

Visual problems, such as crossed eyes and far- or nearsightedness and cataract formation, are higher in those with Down syndrome.

Persons with Down syndrome are prone to repeated ear infections, and they often have mild to moderate hearing loss generally caused by retention of fluid in the inner ear (see Auditory Processing Dysfunction). They often have speech impediments due to enlargement of the tongue.

They also have a 5 to 20 times greater risk than the general population of developing leukemia. According to Charles Epstein, who studies genes related to Down syndrome, someone with Down syndrome has a 1% chance of developing leukemia.

The National Information Center for Children and Youth With Disabilities states that there are more than 50 clinical signs of Down syndrome, but it is rare to find all or even most of the signs in one person. Some common characteristics include the following:

- Speech problems
- Poor muscle tone
- Upward slanting of the eyes with folds of skin at the inner corners
- White spots in the iris of the eye
- Short, broad hands with a single crease across the palm of one or both hands
- Broad feet with short toes
- Flat bridge of the nose
- Short, low-set ears
- Short neck and small head
- Flattened back of the head
- Small oral cavity
- Short, high-pitched cries in infancy
- Large protruding tongues
- Excessive ability for flexing extremities
- Only one flexion furrow on the fifth finger instead of two

Some people with Down syndrome also may have a condition known as Atlantoaxial Instability. This is a misalignment of the top two vertebrae of the neck. This condition makes these individuals more prone to injury if they participate in activities that overextend or flex the neck.

Strategies for Educators

Many students with Down syndrome are being placed into regular academic classrooms. In some instances, they are fully integrated into the regular classroom. In other cases, they might only be integrated for specific courses and times.

Students need to realize that *all* students have feelings. Teachers can encourage students to discuss how they feel when someone teases them versus how they feel when they are given positive feedback.

Only with positive feedback will the disabled student develop a feeling of self-worth. A student who is well-liked by his or her peers and has leadership qualities may be selected to act as a "buddy" for the student. The buddy needs to be made aware that he or she can be instrumental in promoting the acceptance of a student with Down syndrome by the other students. Encourage all students to include the student with Down syndrome in their activities.

Students in the regular classroom need to have an understanding of the student with Down syndrome. To help eliminate the stereotyping of people with Down syndrome, teachers can inform students about well-known people with Down syndrome who have attained success. Many students who are television viewers have seen Chris Burke in the ABC series "Life Goes On," as well as in other shows. Born with Down syndrome, Burke always wanted to be an actor. His own determination and faith helped him achieve his goal. He also coauthored a book with Jo Beth McDaniel, *A Special Kind of Hero: Chris Burke's Own Story* (1991).

Jason Kingsley and Mitchell Levitz, who both have Down syndrome, wrote the book *Count Us In: Growing Up With Down Syndrome* (1994), which challenges the misconceptions and stereotypes surrounding Down syndrome. This book provides students and teachers with insights into the difficulties facing a person with Down syndrome. As Mitchell Levitz stated, "We are trying to erase all the negative attitudes that people had about Down syndrome" (Role Models, 1994).

The student with Down syndrome must be given every opportunity to succeed. Various techniques may be used to reinforce a concept. These include having the student listen to audiotapes and adjusting the length and type of assignment. Teachers should keep in mind that there is a wide variance in the degree of mental retardation in students with Down syndrome, and they should not only set attainable individual goals but encourage students to reach those goals.

The teacher should expect a level of work that is commensurate with the student's ability. It is helpful to provide the student with a notebook to organize the class assignments. Having a notebook prevents the student from losing important information and avoids calling attention to the fact that he or she may have difficulty with regular assignments. Everything possible must be done to maintain and increase feelings of well-being in the student.

Early intervention is important for children with Down syndrome. Research has shown that stimulation during early childhood is necessary for a child with Down syndrome to reach his or her full potential. It is equally important that parents and all school personnel not place limitations on or underestimate the potential capabilities of a child with Down syndrome. Educators should base all intervention strategies on the principles of child development and focus on functional life skills.

There are many community support groups that will aid parents and teachers. For additional information, free directories are available in each state through the National Down Syndrome Society.

Dyslexia

Definition

Dyslexia is a term that applies to a specific reading disability. Medically, it is defined as a condition resulting from neurological, maturational, or genetic causes. The World Federation of Neurology defines dyslexia as "a disorder manifested by difficulty in learning to read despite conventional instruction, adequate intelligence and sociocultural opportunity" (National Institute of Health and Human Development, 1996).

Background

A great deal of research has been done and numerous theories have been developed on the cause of dyslexia. In 1925, Samuel Torrey Orton, a U.S. neuropsychiatrist, was one of the first scientists to investigate dyslexia. He thought the deficiency originated in the visual system. He concluded from his research that dyslexia was the result of a failure of one of the two hemispheres of the brain to dominate language development. Albert Galaburda, a neuroscientist at Harvard Medical School and a world authority on brain anatomy, considers dyslexia to be a problem that results from mistakes in brain development. Several areas in the higher cortex that over time specialize in language development may be abnormal.

Originally, researchers looked for one single cause of dyslexia, but they now believe many factors may be involved. Some believe that dyslexia is caused by either motor or visual defects, such as difficulties in eye tracking, directional scanning, or eye movement. Both visual problems and a lack of cerebral dominance are still considered by many to be valid causes of dyslexia.

Others researchers believe dy:￼ ￼ia is caused by alterations in specific parts of the brain. Recent evidence shows that there is a lag in the brain's maturation and a high degree of left-handedness in people with dyslexia, which may indicate differences in brain function (National Institute of Health and Human Development, 1993).

Still other researchers have theorized that disorders in the structure of the brain may be a factor. This was not an accepted theory until recently, when postmortem examinations showed characteristic disorders of the brain. Although there is an ongoing debate about this theory, some researchers believe it may have some validity.

Research by Paula Tallal and colleagues at the Center for Molecular and Behavioral Neuroscience at Rutgers University suggests that the cause of dyslexia may be the mishearing of fast sounds. Michael Merzenich, a neuroscientist at the University of California, San Francisco, and Tallal are devising new computerized techniques for drawing out or prolonging the sounds of stop consonants (for example, the sound of the letter b) to give children with dyslexia time to hear the consonant. Once they have been able to hear the sounds, it is hoped that the child with dyslexia will gradually develop alternative ways to perceive them.

Some experts believe that dyslexia can be attributed to methods of teaching. For example, they criticize the method of teaching reading by using the whole language approach and claim that students with dyslexia can learn to read by using the phonetic approach. Other experts believe that reading should be taught using a combination of phonics and the whole language approach (National Institute of Health and Human Development, 1993).

Frank R. Vellutino, working at the Child Research and Study Center of the State University of New York at Albany, believes that dyslexia is a language deficiency. Because dyslexic readers can perceive and reproduce letters at the same level as normal readers, the problem may be not the visual coding system but rather one of linguistics. He states, "Far from being a visual problem, dyslexia appears to be the consequence of limited facility in using language to code other types of information" (Vellutino, 1987, p. 34).

Some studies have found that people with dyslexia have no greater incidence of eye problems than those with normal reading ability. Their visual acuity, stereo acuity, ocular alignment, motility fusion status, and refractive errors do not differ from those of the general population.

Because approximately 86% of individuals identified as dyslexic have an auditory language deficit, which prevents the linking of the spoken word with its written equivalent, Mattis (1978) believes the primary factor causing dyslexia is an auditory language deficit.

In contrast to language problems, only 5% of people diagnosed with dyslexia have visual-spatial-motor problems that interfere with sequential organization, scanning, and the perception of temporal and spatial cues. Such problems are common in young children who are just beginning to read and are self-correcting. However, a child with dyslexia whose deficits are undiagnosed and ongoing will miss out on basic instruction in reading.

Dyslexia is commonly associated with the brain's ability to store and retrieve information. Genetic or neurological factors, or both, may be contributing factors. There also appears to be a tendency for more than one member of a family to have dyslexia.

Ninety percent of people with dyslexia are males. Studies show that boys are more impaired in reading than girls and are less capable at language-related tasks. Boys may have fewer linguistic capabilities than girls or be more vulnerable to neurological disorders affecting language development. This possibility may confirm the theory that a true neurological disorder is at the root of dyslexia.

Diagnosis is extremely important to isolate the dyslexic's specific difficulties. Generally, a physician is the first diagnostician to investigate the problem. If indicated, a neurological exam may be given, along with a battery of assessment instruments to find how the specific reading problems are related to the intellectual, achievement, perceptual, motor, linguistic, and adaptive capabilities of the individual. Only after an accurate diagnosis has been made can proper intervention techniques be applied.

Persons with dyslexia have the same wide range of intelligence as the general population. Although a student with dyslexia may lag behind in reading and language skills, with individualized instruction, reading, writing, and spelling can be mastered.

Characteristics

Students with dyslexia may exhibit one or more of the following characteristics:

- Inability to learn and remember words by sight
- Mirror writing—writing backwards so that *help*, for example, would be written *pleh*
- Difficulty in spelling
- Lack of organization of materials
- Difficulty in finding the right words for oral and written communication
- No enjoyment of reading
- Difficulty writing from dictation
- Reversal of letters and words
- Difficulty in storing and retrieving names of printed words
- Poor visual memory for language symbols
- Erratic eye movements while reading
- Auditory processing difficulties
- Difficulty in applying what has been read to social or learning situations
- Illegible handwriting
- Confusing vowels or substituting one consonant (as in *playnate* for *playmate*)
- Clumsiness and awkwardness in using hands

Strategies for Educators

As with other disabilities, the regular classroom students should be given background information about dyslexia. Too often, students believe that individuals with dyslexia are mentally slow because of the academic difficulties they have. To dispel this erroneous belief, teachers can tell students about famous people who had trouble learning to read and write.

Although not scientifically diagnosed as having dyslexia, it would appear that the difficulties experienced by the following would now be attributed to dyslexia: Leonardo da Vinci, Italian Renaissance artist; Hans Christian Andersen, Danish author; Auguste

Rodin, sculptor of *The Thinker*; Woodrow Wilson, president of the United States during World War I; Thomas Edison, American inventor; Winston Churchill, British prime minister during World War II; General George Patton, commander of the American Third Army at the end of World War II; and Harvey Cushing, brain surgeon.

Famous people who have been diagnosed as having dyslexia include George Bush, former president of the United States; Jackie Stewart, race car driver; Duncan Goodhew, Olympic swimmer; Tom Cruise, actor; George Burns, actor; Whoopi Goldberg, actress; Susan Hampshire, actress; Danny Glover, actor; and Cher, actress and singer (National Institute of Health and Human Development, 1996).

Always take the seating arrangements for students with dyslexia into consideration. Seating a student with dyslexia at the front of the class allows the teacher to make sure the student is paying attention and understands what is being taught. With this arrangement, the teacher can provide appropriate work for the student without the rest of the students being made aware of the difference.

Teachers can give students without dyslexia reading selections that demonstrate mirror writing and the halo effect as seen by a student who has dyslexia. When students attempt to read the selections, they will immediately understand the difficulties some students with dyslexia have in reading written material.

When students experience difficulty with reading and math, they should never be told by the teacher to try harder or that they are just lazy. Students with dyslexia are already trying to do their best, and the teacher's comments will only lead to more frustration and an eventual abandonment of the task.

The teacher should never force a student with dyslexia to read aloud to the class. It is better to let the student follow along silently as others read aloud or to let him or her tape-record the reading selection. Follow-up activities that are primarily verbal can eliminate a great deal of stress for the student.

The student with dyslexia often has great difficulty producing written work. Educators should not compare this work with the work of the rest of the class. Offer praise for any written accomplishment, regardless of how slight it might be. The teacher should be flexible and allow the student to tape-record reports or use a word-processing program. On occasion, arrangements may also be made for the other students in the class to do the same. This will help the student with dyslexia to feel less "different."

Early recognition of the problem minimizes the frustrations of dyslexic students. They need praise and positive feedback, as do the other students in the classroom.

Emotional Disturbance

Definition

The Individuals with Disabilities Education Act (IDEA, 1990) currently defines serious emotional disturbance as follows:

> A condition exhibiting one or more of the following charac-
> teristics over a long period of time and to a marked degree,
> which adversely affects educational performance: an inability to
> learn that cannot be explained by intellectual, sensory, or health
> factors; an inability to build or maintain satisfactory interper-
> sonal relations with peers and teachers; a general pervasive
> mood of unhappiness or depression; or a tendency to develop
> physical symptoms or fears associated with personal or school
> problems.

Background

Emotionally disturbed and *severely emotionally disturbed* are terms that are used in the law. However, the terms *behaviorally disturbed* or *behavioral disorder* are often used when referring to a student who has emotional difficulties. To avoid confusion, the legal term *emotionally disturbed* will be used in this book, even though the term is a broad one. It must be remembered that many people who display emotional disturbances of varying degrees at one time or another do not fall in this category. At some time during their development, many children who do not have emotional disturbances may display behaviors associated with individuals who are emotionally disturbed. To fit the definition as stated, the duration and intensity of the disturbance and whether it impacts or impedes the student's ability to achieve education goals have to be taken into consideration.

There is a large variance among the estimated number of children and youth who have emotional disturbances. According to the American Psychological Association, approximately 15% of school-age children are in need of some type of therapy. In the 1990 Twelfth Annual Report to Congress, the United States Department of Education stated that for the school year 1988–1989, 377,295 children and youth with emotional disturbances were provided services in the public schools. This figure did not include the many preschool children who may have emotional disturbances but are not so classified.

Various factors have been suggested as possible causes of emotional disturbances, such as genetic deficiency, neurological impairment, brain injury, a chemical imbalance, nutritional deficiencies, and the use of alcohol or drugs by the parents.

Divorce, the death or birth of sibling, moving, changing schools, and peer pressure are but a few of the many external events that may lead to an emotional disturbance in a child. When children grow up in unpredictable, stressful surroundings, inappropriate behavior is not only learned but constantly reinforced. Such children may either act out or repress their feelings. Both types of behavior, if they continue for a long time or form part of a larger pattern of behavior, can be considered to be those of emotionally disturbed individuals.

When one suspects that a child is emotionally disturbed, it is important to consider one's own personal perception of the child. The teacher's tolerance for misbehavior should be examined. To accurately identify children who are emotionally disturbed, testing and observation by trained medical professionals or psychologists is required.

Characteristics

The following are some basic characteristics and behaviors seen in children who have emotional disturbances:

- Hyperactivity
- Short attention span
- Impulsiveness
- Aggression (acting out, fighting)
- Self-injurious behavior
- Withdrawal from interaction with others
- Immaturity (inappropriate crying, temper tantrums)
- Poor coping skills
- Learning problems

Children with the most serious emotional disturbances exhibit distorted thinking, excessive anxiety, bizarre motor acts, and abnormal mood swings, and are sometimes identified as having a severe psychosis or schizophrenia.

Strategies for Educators

The use of behavior modifications to shape the behaviors of the student with positive reinforcement may improve the student's attitudes and behaviors to meet the classroom expectations. However, it is important for the teacher to remember that self-management should always be encouraged.

Structure in a classroom is of primary importance for an emotionally disturbed student. The teacher must define clear and explicit limits and consequences for unacceptable behaviors. The student must understand the consequences of undesirable behaviors; teachers should always and consistently carry out the expected consequences.

Teachers should work at developing a good rapport with the emotionally disturbed student. The teacher can take advantage of many opportunities throughout the day to reinforce feelings of self-worth in the student. Simple things, such as eye contact, smiling, praise for good work, or close proximity, can help nurture the relationship.

The teacher should also be alert to any sign that the student may be experiencing an emotional difficulty or crisis and may be on the verge of losing control. The teacher should provide a preestablished "time-out" area or place where the student can go. This will help the student regain his or her composure and sidetrack an episode. The student should not be required to ask permission; instead, the student can be alerted by a preestablished sign from the teacher.

The teacher can sometimes prevent problems simply by diverting the student's attention. Without alerting the other students to the situation, the teacher can quietly remind the emotionally disturbed student of the consequences of a certain misbehavior. This will help prevent the unwanted behavior from taking place. Many of the suggestions for helping an ADHD student are also applicable for the student who is emotionally disturbed.

A student whose behavior is disruptive and apt to cause physical harm to other students may need to be removed from the classroom. This may require the assistance of other school personnel.

If the student tries to or is expected to change too many types of behavior at one time, he or she will likely experience feelings of frustration and failure. Teachers must go slowly when attempting any type of behavioral change. Often, for the teacher, dealing with a student who is emotionally disturbed also requires a change in one's own behavior patterns. Difficult as it may be, it may be best to ignore, when possible, the undesirable behavior. Annoying behavior that gets attention tends to be repeated, whereas praising and rewarding provides the kind of attention that will lead to improvement.

All persons dealing with an emotionally disturbed child should keep in mind what Mark Twain said: "Habit is habit, and not to be flung out of the window by any man, but coaxed downstairs a step at a time" (quoted in Phillips, 1993, p. 153).

Epilepsy

Definition

Epilepsy is a chronic condition that is a sign or symptom of an underlying neurological disorder. It consists of recurrent seizures of varying degrees of intensity and duration. These seizures are the result of a temporary alteration in one or more brain functions. According to the Epilepsy Foundation of America (1985a, 1985b, 1987, 1988), a person's consciousness, movement, or actions may be altered for a short time when the brain cells are not working properly. Although epilepsy is sometimes called a seizure disorder, the two terms are not synonymous. A person can suffer a seizure without being epileptic. Isolated and provoked seizures, as might occur with the use of alcohol or drugs, are not epilepsy. Persons with epilepsy have recurring, unprovoked seizures.

Background

Epilepsy is one of the oldest known brain disorders. Reference was made to epilepsy 2,000 years B.C.E. as well as in ancient Greek writings. However, it was not until the middle of the 19th century that epilepsy began to be studied scientifically.

Throughout history, society has regarded people with epilepsy in different ways. Ignorance of its causes gave way to many erroneous beliefs. In some cultures, individuals with epilepsy were thought to have divine or demonic power. Epilepsy also was thought to be contagious and the cause of mental retardation or mental illness. Unfortunately, there are some who, to this day, believe these myths. Such erroneous beliefs have created a social stigma surrounding epilepsy that has plagued both individuals with epilepsy and their families.

Estimates are that 1% to 2% of the population have or have had some form of epilepsy. It is possible that there is an inherited tendency to have epilepsy. According to the National Information Center for Children and Youth With Disabilities (1990b), about 2 million Americans have epilepsy. Of the 100,000 new cases that develop each year, three quarters of them involve children and adolescents. Generally, epileptic seizures start before the age of 21.

According to the Comprehensive Epilepsy Program of the University of Minnesota (1980), more than 50% of all people with epilepsy can control their seizures with medicine, and another 20% to 30% have improved control of seizures with medication. A small number of children are not helped or may become worse using medication, but medication controls seizure attacks in the majority of epileptic children. Fortunately, children may outgrow epilepsy and require no medication for the disorder later in life.

The causes of epilepsy are numerous: birth trauma, brain infection, head injury, brain tumor, stroke, drug intoxication, interruption of blood flow to the brain, or a metabolic imbalance in the body. Environmental factors can also bring on an epileptic seizure. In some cases, they can be triggered by sudden changes from light to dark or vice versa, flashing lights, loud noises, or monotonous sounds. Withdrawal from alcohol and illicit drugs can also bring out an underlying epileptic disorder. Seizures are unpredictable and nonhuman animals as well as people can have them.

Sometimes, for no apparent reason, seizures develop that are unrelated to epilepsy. Pseudoepileptic seizures can occur in people who do not have diagnosed epilepsy, and the symptoms may be much like those of an epileptic seizure. These attacks may be brought on by a conscious or unconscious desire for attention and care. When seizures occur so frequently that they interfere with academic learning, they are considered to be a health impairment that makes the student eligible for special education placement.

Seizures may affect intelligence because a prolonged seizure reduces the oxygen in the brain during the episode. However, impaired intellectual functioning in a developmentally delayed person with epilepsy is usually not caused by the epilepsy, but is rather a result of the developmental delay. Generally, people with epilepsy have normal intelligence.

Because there are more than 30 different types of seizures, the International League Against Epilepsy has replaced the outdated classifications of the different types with two main categories—*partial* and *generalized*. A seizure is considered to be partial if the electrical activity involves only a limited area of the brain. If the electrical discharge involves the entire brain, the seizure is considered to be generalized. Each of these classifications is further divided into different subdivisions. The partial and generalized categories are now generally accepted by the medical community.

Characteristics

The National Information Center for Children and Youth With Disabilities (1990b) states that, in general, the signs of epilepsy include episodes of staring or unexplained periods of unresponsiveness, involuntary movement of arms and legs, fainting spells with incontinence, odd sounds, distorted perceptions, and episodic feelings of fear that cannot be explained. Blackouts or confused memory can also be signs of epilepsy.

Generalized Seizures

Characteristics can vary, depending on the nature of the epilepsy. A prolonged seizure can last for many hours. A *tonic-clonic* seizure, formerly called *grand mal*, is a generalized seizure that usually lasts 30 seconds to several minutes. (If a person has multiple seizures of this type or a seizure that lasts longer than 5 minutes, medical attention is definitely indicated.) A tonic-clonic seizure can be very unnerving to the onlooker. There is a cry and an ensuing loss of consciousness. The body becomes rigid and the person falls unconscious to the ground. This is followed by jerky muscle contractions. There may be a loss of bladder and bowel control. The breathing becomes shallow and very irregular or temporarily ceases. After regaining consciousness, the person may not recall the events of the seizure but usually will be very fatigued and require rest.

Another form of generalized seizure is an *absence seizure*, often referred to as a *petit mal.* During the seizure, the person is out of touch with reality but returns to normal when the seizure is over. Petit mal seizures start with a blank stare and end abruptly. There can be chewing movements of the mouth and rapid blinking, but it is not accompanied by abnormal movements of the body. The episode can last a few seconds to half a minute or so. It is sometimes accompanied by a momentary loss of consciousness, but it can also go completely unnoticed by bystanders. This type of seizure can occur hundreds of times daily and is often mistaken for daydreaming or lack of attention by the teacher.

Partial Seizures

Partial seizures are categorized as simple or complex. Simple partial seizures are also called *sensory* or *Jacksonian seizures.* Simple partial seizures can occur without warning and may last several minutes. There may be abnormal tingling sensations and twitching. If the twitching spreads slowly from one part of the body to another, it eventually may involve the whole body and lead to a convulsive seizure. The person may have unexplained feelings of anger, joy, and fear, as well as a distinct feeling of nausea. Although there is no loss of consciousness and the person retains all awareness, he or she may hear and see things that are nonexistent.

In complex partial seizures, also known as *psychomotor* or *temporal lobe seizures,* the person becomes dazed and may not respond to others. His or her actions are inappropriate, out of character, or uncoordinated. Some individuals may pick at their clothing or take their clothes off, and others may fumble with buttons or smack their lips. They may experience sudden fear, try to run, and struggle against any kind of restraint. As with the simple partial seizure, there may be distortions of hearing or seeing. After the seizure, there is no recall of the events that occurred during the attack. Although partial seizures may begin in a limited area of the brain, the disturbance may spread and affect the entire brain, thus leading to a generalized seizure (Epilepsy Foundation of America, 1988).

Strategies for Educators

All educators should be made aware of students who have a history of epilepsy. Vital information can be obtained by checking students' cumulative and health records. Parents can also provide additional information about the type of seizure their child has and its frequency. Even if seizures are controlled by medication, school personnel should be aware that there may be side effects from the medication. Document any changes in physical or intellectual functioning, and keep the child's parent and doctor informed of such changes.

The teacher can be instrumental in helping nondisabled students understand what epilepsy is and in alleviating their misconceptions and fears. It is sufficient for younger students to know that seizures do not hurt and are generally of short duration; older students should be taught the nature of epilepsy and the effect it has on the student who has seizures.

Students may wonder why the teacher does not try to stop a student's seizure. They need to understand that once a seizure has started, it should not be interrupted. The seizure must be allowed to run its course.

When someone has a seizure (with the exception of the absence and petit mal forms), the following actions should be taken:

- Keep calm and do not try to revive the student.
- Ease the student to the floor and put something soft under the person's head.
- Turn the student on one side to keep the airway open.
- Allow fluid in the mouth to drain.
- Remove any hard, sharp, or hot objects from the immediate area.
- Do not attempt to restrain *any* movements of the student.
- Loosen the student's clothing.
- Do not give the student anything to drink or swallow during the seizure.
- Do not force the mouth open or put anything in the student's mouth.
- Do not hold the student's tongue. He or she will not swallow it.
- If the student walks aimlessly during the seizure, clear the area of potentially dangerous objects.

During the seizure attack, the student's breathing may be shallow. Because of the lack of oxygen, the lips and skin may have a bluish tinge. There is no cause for alarm unless the breathing ceases. It is then necessary to immediately check to see if there is something blocking the student's airway and remove it. Artificial respiration also may be needed.

After the seizure is over, the person may be extremely tired and should be allowed to rest.

As with other emergency drills, such as fire drills, it is helpful if students role play in advance and demonstrate what should be done if another student has a seizure.

Many epileptics have led very successful lives, and the teacher should provide students with information about them. This also will give students an opportunity for research and language activities. The following is a partial list of famous people who had or who have epilepsy: Alexander the Great, military leader and king of Macedonia; Julius Caesar, Roman statesman and general; Buddha, religious philosopher; Mohammed, founder of the Moslem religion; Charles Dickens, English novelist; George Handel, German composer; Hector Berlioz, French composer; Paganini, Italian violinist and composer; Ludwig van Beethoven, German composer; Vincent van Gogh, Dutch painter; Sir Isaac Newton, English mathematician and natural philosopher; Marion Clignet, champion cyclist; Deborah McFadden, Commissioner, Administration on Developmental Disabilities; the late Margeaux Hemingway, actress; Patty Wilson, long-distance runner; Richard Burton, actor; Gary Howatt, professional hocky player; John Considine, actor; and Buddy Bell, professional baseball player.

An epileptic student's seizures may interfere with the ability to learn. A student whose seizures are characterized by a brief period of fixed staring may miss out on what is being said. Teachers must take this into consideration.

Individuals with epilepsy should not be overprotected, as this hinders their psychological and social growth. For epileptic people to feel more confident about themselves and accept their condition, they need to be treated with respect and acceptance.

Fetal Alcohol Syndrome

Definition

Fetal alcohol syndrome (FAS) refers to fetal developmental defects that result from a woman's consumption of alcohol during pregnancy. In cases in which these defects are not severe enough to meet all the criteria for an FAS diagnosis, the term *fetal alcohol effects* (FAE) is used.

Background

Since the beginning of the 18th century, physicians and researchers in England and France have reported the harmful effects of maternal alcohol consumption on the fetus. In 1973, a group of scientists at the University of Washington, Seattle, coined the term *fetal alcohol syndrome* to describe the characteristic birth defects of the affected infants. In 1980, the Fetal Alcohol Study Group of the Research Society on Alcoholism outlined standards for an FAS diagnosis. As stated in *Alcohol, Tobacco, and Other Drugs May Harm the Unborn* (Cook, Petersen, & Moore, 1990), these standards require that an infant have at least one feature from each of the following categories in order to be classified as having FAS:

1. Pre- and postnatal growth retardation, with abnormally small-for-age weight, length, and or head circumference
2. Central nervous systems disorders, with signs of abnormal brain functioning and delays in behavioral development or intellectual development, or both
3. At least two of the following abnormal craniofacial features: small head, small eyes or short eye openings, or a poorly developed groove above the upper lip, thin upper lip, or flattened mid-facial area (p. 17)

The standards for an FAS diagnosis do not include other abnormalities that sometimes occur. Babies who had been prenatally exposed to alcohol and have other birth defects, but who have only a few of the official accepted signs of FAS, may be categorized as having suspected FAE.

Although it is not known exactly how often FAS occurs in babies, the range in the United States has been estimated as 1 to 5 per 1,000 live births. Researchers in European cities who have studied the effects of women's alcohol consumption on infants during pregnancy offer comparable rates.

According to the U.S. Department of Health and Human Services, risk factors for having a baby with FAS include "the mother's persistent drinking throughout pregnancy, a greater number of alcohol-related problems, and a larger number of previous births" (Cook, Petersen, & Moore, 1990, p. 18). In addition, women who had previous babies with FAS had an increased risk of having another baby with FAS in the future.

Studies also have been conducted on the effects on the fetus of paternal drinking. As stated in *Alcohol Health & Research World* (Cicero, 1994), paternal alcohol consumption may have a direct effect on fetal development. In addition, there are indications that paternal drinking may contribute to cognitive and biochemical disturbances in the fetus.

It is difficult to ascertain the exact amount of alcohol that can safely be consumed by the woman during pregnancy. Even very small amounts of alcohol may be harmful and increase the risk of a miscarriage or congenital birth defects. Infants with neurobehavioral deficits and intrauterine growth retardation have been born to women who stated that they were only moderate drinkers. In evaluating this statement, it is important to take into account that individuals may underreport their alcohol consumption. In some cases, women who drank heavily during pregnancy have borne babies with no signs of FAS. However, these babies are the exception rather than the rule. Many times, women bear infants who have FAE with no apparent outward symptoms, and it is only later that the symptoms become evident. The American Medical Association states that there is no safe level of alcohol consumption for women during pregnancy. Most authorities and the medical profession advise abstinence from consuming alcohol during pregnancy.

High doses of alcohol interfere with the passage of amino acids across the placenta and the conversion of amino acids into proteins. It appears that the breakdown products in alcohol of ethanol and its metabolite, acetaldehyde, alter fetal development by "disrupting cell differentiation and cell growth." The American Medical Association also states that the immature and underdeveloped fetus's organs break down alcohol much more slowly than the pregnant woman's, causing a higher level of toxins in the fetus.

In the book *The Broken Cord* (1989), Michael Dorris writes, "There have been babies born whose skin, the whole baby, smells like wine. It's like they're pickled and the amniotic fluid is saturated with alcohol" (p. 158).

Any drug taken during pregnancy crosses the placenta (DeVane, 1991, p. 18). Alcohol consumption not only increases the chances of producing a baby with FAS or FAE but also contributes to stress, lack of stability, and a dysfunctional family.

Characteristics

Almost one fifth of FAS infants die during their first few weeks of life. Those who survive usually are physically and mentally impaired in varying degrees. The following are some of the characteristics commonly found in FAS infants and children. Not all of the characteristics listed are found in every FAS case.

Physical Abnormalities	*Behavioral Deficits*
Small infant size	Hyperactivity
Small head circumference	Short- and long-term memory
Low, narrow forehead	problems
Small mid-face	Learning disabilities
Thin and long upper lip	Extreme nervousness
Brain damage	Impulsiveness
Heart defects	Inability to understand
Delayed dental development	outcomes of behavior
Joint and limb irregularities	Slow academic progress
Abnormal central nervous	
system	
Hearing impairment	
Slow growth after birth	
Mental retardation	
Fine motor dysfunction	
Seizures	

Strategies for Educators

The many disorders exhibited by FAS and FAE students (e.g., ADHD, emotional disturbances, and other impairments) require teachers to make various educational modifications. Suggestions for teaching FAS or FAE students with multiple disabilities can be found under specific disabilities in this book (see, for example, ADHD and emotional disturbances).

Because the child's future total environment is unpredictable, it is difficult to determine what the long-term developmental effects of the drug use will be on the infant. However, the importance of family, school, peers, and community cannot be underestimated. It is only with support and understanding that the FAS and FAE child's potential will be tapped.

With the use of alcohol increasing, one can expect that an increasing number of babies will be born with FAS or FAE. The importance of educating teachers, students, and parents about the dangers is clear.

Head Injury

Definition

The Individuals with Disabilities Education Act (IDEA) defines *traumatic brain injury* (TBI) as an acquired injury to the brain caused by an external force resulting in total or partial functional disability or psychosocial impairment that adversely affects a child's educational performance. The IDEA now includes TBI as a separate disability category (National Information Center for Children and Youth With Disabilities, 1995).

Background

A *closed head injury* is generally the result of a sharp acceleration and deceleration of the head that results in the brain being shaken. This stress pulls apart the nerve fibers and results in damage to the neurofibers that send messages to all parts of the body. This type of injury puts stress on the brain stem, which is the lowest section of the brain where 10 of the 12 pairs of cranial nerves connect. These nerves automatically control basic functions of the body, such as eye reflexes, breathing, facial movements, and heartbeat. All messages going to the brain pass through the brain stem first.

In contrast to a closed head injury, an *open head injury* is the result of a head trauma that damages a focal point in the brain, which in turn causes specific problems for the individual. For example, an individual may have difficulty producing speech but have no difficulty putting thoughts on paper. In any open head injury, there is always the potential for serious infection, because of dirt or a foreign object being implanted in the brain. If the skull is fractured, there is a danger that bone fragments may be driven into the brain. A severe blow to the head may bruise brain tissue, resulting in brain cell death, or cause the blood vessels to tear, causing a brain hemorrhage.

Although many people sustain some type of head injury at least once in their lifetime, they seldom require treatment by a neurosurgeon. However, according to the National Head Injury Foundation, more than 2 million people sustain traumatic brain injuries each year, with 500,000 requiring hospital admission. It is also estimated that every 15 seconds someone receives a head injury in the United States. Estimates are that each year 75,000 to 100,000 will die, either at the time of the injury or within several hours of the injury. It is also estimated that 70,000 to 90,000 survivors of traumatic head injuries will sustain lifelong loss of function and that 2,000 will remain in a persistent vegetative state (National Head Injury Foundation, 1989).

TBI is one of the leading causes of death or disability in children and young adults. Between the ages of 15 and 24, twice as many males than females suffer serious head injuries. Sixty-four percent of infant head injuries are due to child abuse. In the United States, 50,000 children sustain bicycle-related head injuries every year. Overall, motor vehicle accidents cause one half of all traumatic head injuries, falls make up 21%, assaults and violence 12%, and sports and recreation 10% (National Institute of Neurological Disorders and Stroke, 1989).

Generally, an individual who suffers a severe head injury will have to undergo intensive treatment for 5 to 10 years, sometimes for a lifetime. The effects of a head injury are both physical and psychological, and they can change the individual's present and future life dramatically.

Characteristics

The characteristics of TBIs are as wide and varied as the individuals who sustain the injuries. The impairments may be temporary or permanent and may include the following:

- Speech, vision, and other sensory disadvantages
- Fine motor coordination impairment
- Muscle spasticity
- Paralysis on one or both sides of the body
- Seizure disorders
- Short- and long-term memory impairment
- Short attention span

- Poor reading and writing skills
- Impairment of judgment
- Mood swings and depression
- Emotional- and impulse-control impairment
- Difficulties in relating to others
- Lowered self-esteem

Children who have suffered a TBI often remember what they were like prior to the brain injury, which may cause many emotional and psychosocial difficulties. Although the rates of emotional and social development vary from individual to individual, all people with TBI must deal with both physical and social problems. One factor remains constant: The individual has to completely restructure his or her life.

Strategies for Educators

Many education professionals are unaware of the consequences of childhood head injury. Often, students with TBI are inappropriately classified as having learning disabilities, emotional disturbances, or mental retardation. A thorough evaluation is necessary in order to develop an appropriate individualized education program to meet the special needs of the student with TBI.

Teachers should provide background information on head injuries to all students. Students should be informed about the many possible consequences of sustaining a head injury, followed by a discussion of preventive safety practices.

To maximize the comfort and productivity of a student with a head injury, educators can apply the same suggestions given earlier in the book for creating an environment that is as free from distraction as possible for the ADHD student, making the necessary adjustments based on the severity of the injury.

TBI is considered to be a "silent epidemic" because the physical signs of it may not always be visible. However, TBI generally results in various disabilities. Depending on the particular disability, other factors need to be considered.

A student with TBI may, for example, have difficulty with orientation and require supervision walking between the classroom and restroom. A "buddy" system can be advantageous in such cases. Students with TBI may also exhibit other physical disabilities or impairments, and specific suggestions for handling them may be found under those disabilities in this book.

To meet the special needs of a student with TBI, the teacher will have to readjust the goals and expectations for the student. If the student's long-term memory is impaired, he or she will often need to review previously learned material. If there is short-term memory impairment, what was learned the day before may be forgotten and need to be taught again. Also, teachers must assess whether the student with TBI can only follow one-step instructions or is capable of understanding a sequence of two or more directions.

Educators will find that using a multisensory approach is advantageous for the brain-injured student as well as for other students. They should demonstrate new tasks and give examples to illustrate ideas and concepts. Reinforce by repetition, and when giving instructions, avoid the use of figurative language.

The teacher of a student with TBI should never focus on the student's disabling injury. This only diminishes the student's self-esteem and possibly may lead to a demeaning attitude on the part of other classmates. Instead, the teacher must focus on the student's strengths to maximize his or her learning potential.

Students with TBI need an accepting and positive environment. Even though there may be a complete change in the behavior of students with head injuries, they should be treated with dignity and respect.

Advances in treatment and rehabilitation have helped many who have sustained brain injury. Communication among the medical profession, special education team, and parents of the child who sustained a brain injury is extremely important. With the care and positive support both of professionals and family, many with TBI are able to surmount their difficulties and lead a rewarding life.

Hearing Impairment

Definition

A hearing-impaired person is considered to be *deaf* if the sense of hearing is nonfunctional for the ordinary purposes of life, or *hard of hearing* when the sense of hearing is defective but functional, with or without a hearing aid. A hearing impairment should not be confused with auditory processing, which is the inability to interpret auditory stimuli and is not the result of a hearing loss.

Background

An estimated 21 million Americans have some degree of hearing impairment. Nearly 4,500,000 Americans who are hard of hearing wear hearing aids to compensate for their hearing loss, and the National Information Center on Deafness estimates that between 350,000 and 2 million people are deaf. However, most of these people are older than age 65.

Both hereditary and environmental factors play a role in deafness. Total deafness, which is rare, is usually congenital. In about 50% of all cases of deafness, genetic factors are a probable cause. Partial deafness, ranging from moderate to severe, is generally the result of an ear disease, injury, or degeneration of the hearing mechanism with age (National Information Center on Deafness, Gallaudet University, 1989).

All hearing impairments fall into the categories of *sensorineural, conductive,* or *mixed.* Each category has different problems and different possibilities for medical and nonmedical remediation.

Sensorineural hearing loss is the result of damage to the delicate sensory hair cells or the nerves of the inner ear. This type of loss can be due to an inherited fault in a chromosome, as well as to birth injury or damage to the developing fetus, such as when a pregnant woman contracts rubella. Subjection to loud noise for prolonged periods increases the pressure in the labyrinth of the ear, which can result in a sensorineural hearing loss. The loss can range from mild to profound. Even with amplification to increase the sound level, there can be distortion. In some cases, the distortion is so great that the use of a hearing aid is not beneficial.

Conductive hearing loss usually affects all frequencies of hearing but generally does not result in a severe loss of hearing. It can be caused by diseases or obstructions in the outer or middle ear. Conductive deafness can also be caused by damage to the eardrum or middle ear due to pressure, injury, a middle-ear infection, or surgery on the ear. Conductive hearing loss due to ear wax blocking the outer ear canal is common in adults. In children, otitis media, a middle-ear infection, is the most common cause of this type of deafness. Most people with this type of hearing loss can be helped medically, surgically, or by the use of a hearing aid.

Hearing tests measure how well a person can hear across the entire range of sound frequencies. Both hertz and decibels are used in hearing tests to find out the degree of loss. A sound's intensity or loudness is measured in decibels (dB), and its frequency or pitch is measured in hertz (Hz). The threshold of hearing is 0 dB. The larger the number, the louder the sound it represents. For example, 18 dB represents the loudness of a soft whisper at 18 feet away, in contrast to 108 dB, which represents the sound of a jet taking off 200 feet away.

The following number system classifies the degree of hearing impairment in decibels:

25–40 dB = mild
41–55 dB = moderate
56–70 dB = moderately severe
71–90 dB = severe
91+ dB = profound

A hertz is a unit of frequency equal to one cycle per second. High-pitched sounds have a higher number of cycles per second and low-pitched sounds have a lower number of cycles per second.

The majority of children with impaired hearing have already acquired some basic sentence patterns and verbal information when they enter school. They need a symbol and communication system that will allow them to be effective and efficient in their social interactions.

American Sign Language (ASL) is one of a variety of communication systems used by hearing-impaired people in the United States. It uses the visual medium rather than the aural. Handshakes, facial expressions, and the orientation of the body's movements convey meaning. ASL is different from English in that it is a universal language with its own vocabulary, grammar, and language patterns.

Signed English, also known as *Pidgin Signed English* utilizes both finger spelling and ASL. *Finger spelling* is a manual alphabet. It is similar to writing in the air rather than on paper. Finger spelling is generally used in conjunction with ASL. Finger spelling used in combination with spoken English is referred to as the Rochester method. It is presented in the exact word order as in English, as a direct translation.

In *speech reading,* sometimes referred to as *lipreading,* the deaf person watches the speaker's lips, facial expression, and gestures. However, there are difficulties with this form of communication because many English words are not visible on the lips and half of them look like something else. However, some individuals with a degree of hearing impairment have developed great skill in lipreading.

Cued speech uses eight hand shapes in four possible positions to supplement the information that is visible on the lips of the speaker. Hand cues signal the difference between sounds that look alike on the lips. For example, the letters *p* and *b* look the same. Using cued speech when communicating with someone whose hearing is impaired helps the person identify the correct word.

Oral communication refers to the use of speech, residual hearing, and lipreading. Some researchers believe that all deaf children may have functional residual hearing. Oral communication relies heavily on an auditory and visual approach to help people acquire and develop language through their residual hearing.

Simultaneous communication uses both spoken words and finger spelling. The person who has a hearing impairment lip-reads along with the signs and finger spelling of the speaker.

Total communication uses all possible methods of communication. Many now believe that the approach that works best for an individual with a hearing impairment should be used.

Characteristics

People with a mild degree of hearing loss may have normal speech patterns, and their hearing impairment often may go undetected. A student with a mild degree of hearing loss may have difficulty hearing faint speech as well as speech at a distance. Often, the student with a mild hearing loss will be inattentive and therefore be considered disobedient. If language development is lacking, the student may have difficulty understanding abstract ideas and concepts.

If there is a moderate loss of hearing and no hearing aid is used, a student may miss much of what is spoken and be unable to participate in class discussions. If conditions are favorable, such students may be able to understand conversational speech within a distance of 3 to 5 feet. Often, they are able to hear vowels in conversational speech, but some of the consonants may be heard imperfectly or not at all.

A child who has a moderately severe hearing loss and does not use a hearing aid will hear very little conversational speech. Because speech develops as the direct result of hearing, a child with a moderately severe hearing loss may have defective speech, minimal expressive vocabulary, and inadequate language structure.

When there is a severe loss of hearing, most ordinary environmental sounds are not heard, but the person may sense loud noises and respond to loud voices. Some who are profoundly deaf may be able to hear loud sounds and loud voices very close to the ear. However, the person's speech will be meaningless. In the early developmental years, a child may be entirely without words. He or she may have vocalizations but few sounds will be recognizable as words.

Technological advances and telecommunications devices for the deaf, such as teletypewriter machines, have made it possible for the hearing impaired to increase their independence. Telecaption adapters that enable a person to read dialogue and captions on the TV screen can now be added to television sets or purchased along with the TV.

Signaling devices or vibrating signals may be added to the already existing auditory signal. When the doorbell rings, these devices flash to alert the person who is hearing impaired. Some alarm clocks have a flashing light or vibrating signal. These devices are also used to alert the person with a hearing impairment when a telephone rings, a baby cries, or a smoke alarm goes off. These are just a few of the devices available to help people who are hearing impaired. Technology is steadily advancing and innovative designs are continually being created to improve the quality of life for people with hearing impairments.

Strategies for Educators

For peers to appreciate what it is like to be hearing impaired, the teacher can purchase inexpensive ear plugs for the students, ask the students to place these plugs in theirs, and then proceed with the lessons. Students will quickly realize the difficulties encountered by the hearing impaired. In addition, most special education departments have tape recordings available that demonstrate what the hearing impaired hear at the different levels of hearing loss.

Many educators mistakenly believe that they must speak very loudly to a hearing-impaired student. It is best to speak in a normal conversational voice. Speaking slowly and distinctly is indispensable in helping the student with a hearing impairment to understand what you say. Of course, this does not pertain to the person who is profoundly deaf.

Often, teachers have a tendency to overexaggerate mouth movements when speaking to a student with a hearing impairment. This only confuses the student and makes it impossible to lip-read. When speaking, the teacher should always face the student. It is helpful to write assignments on the chalkboard, but the teacher should remember to turn around to face the student before explaining the assignment.

Educators should consider the seating arrangement for a student with a hearing impairment. The student should be seated within 10 feet of the teacher; this will allow the student to lip-read and also interpret visual clues.

The lighting in the room should not fall directly on the face of the student, as this may make it difficult for him or her to observe the teacher. It is also harder for the student to lip-read or interpret the teacher's visual clues if the teacher stands in front of a window or light.

Provide handouts on key points to a student with a hearing impairment. This will help him or her to follow instructions. When possible, this material should be given to the support person who is also responsible for the education of the student and who, in turn, can provide the reinforcement the student needs to gain a sense of confidence when included in the regular class. Provision can be made to have an interpreter for the hearing impaired student in the classroom. An interpreter will give additional assistance to the student who is hearing impaired and be of great help to the regular teacher.

It is beneficial for all students to study prominent people who were hearing impaired yet successful, such as Thomas Edison and Helen Keller, who also was blind.

Our society is composed of many people who have been deaf since birth or who have lost their hearing later in life. They are found in many occupations. Unfortunately, as a group, they are underemployed. The situation is changing as understanding and compassion for people with hearing impairments grows. Educators and society as a whole can do much to increase opportunities for them.

Learning Disabilities

Definition

The term *learning disability* is currently used to describe a dysfunction that interferes with someone's ability to store, process, or produce information. The IDEA defines a learning disability as a "disorder in one or more of the basic psychological processes involved in understanding or in using spoken or written language, which may manifest itself in an imperfect ability to listen, think, speak, read, write, spell or to do mathematical calculations" (National Information Center for Children and Youth with Disabilities, 1992). According to this law, learning disabilities do not include learning problems that are primarily the result of visual, hearing, or motor disabilities; mental retardation; or environmental, cultural, or economic disadvantage.

Background

A review of the literature reveals a number of different terms that are being used to refer to learning disabilities. This is not surprising, because the problem spans many disciplines, including special education, psychology, speech correction, child development, neurology, and medicine.

The many different estimates of the number of children with learning disabilities—ranging from 1% to 30% of the general population—reflect the variation in the definition of learning disabilities. In 1987, the Interagency Committee on Learning Disabilities concluded that 5% to 10% was a reasonable estimate. The U.S. Department of Education reported in 1991 that nearly 5% of all school-age children were receiving special education. In the 1989–1990 school year, more than 2 million children with learning disabilities were being served.

A child who is doing poorly in school may appear to be lazy or emotionally disturbed, but the problems may be the result of a learning disability and require intervention. It is essential to identify students with learning disabilities as early as possible to prevent or alleviate the frustration and failure such students experience. A collaborative team approach will help facilitate the child's overall development.

A determination of the student's intelligence is needed to ascertain whether the child is performing at his or her potential. A discrepancy between the student's ability and actual performance may indicate a learning disability. Because students require different learning strategies depending on the type of learning disability they have, assessment is essential to obtaining accurate information that will help students, parents, and the teacher to understand and help the student learn how to overcome the effects of having a learning disability. The identification of students with learning disabilities may require observation and diagnostic testing by both education and medical professionals.

Characteristics

Individuals with learning disabilities may have problems with reading comprehension, speech, writing, or reasoning ability. The following characteristics may be exhibited by students with learning disabilities:

- Awkward use of pencil and scissors
- Distractibility
- Hyperactivity
- Perceptual coordination problems
- Impulsiveness
- Lack of organizational skills
- Low tolerance for frustrations and problems
- Difficulty in reasoning
- Difficulty in one or more academic areas
- Low self-esteem
- Problems with social relationships
- Difficulty beginning or completing tasks
- Uneven and unpredictable test performance
- Aural sequential memory deficit
- Visual sequential memory deficit
- Auditory processing difficulties
- Visual-motor coordination problems
- Dysfunction in the neurological system

Characteristics of those who have learning disabilities may vary from individual to individual, but one common aspect is that a learning-disabled person has an average to above-average IQ. There is also a demonstrated discrepancy between intellectual ability and achievement in one or more academic areas. Depending on the nature of the learning disability, the student may be quick to learn some skills and slower at other skills.

Unfortunately, students who are learning disabled are sometimes mistakenly considered to be slow learners and to show little academic growth. It is important to check the academic records of a student to ascertain what the academic profile reveals. A slow learner will depict a low, flat profile of growth, whereas the learning-disabled student's profile will show a markedly uneven pattern of progress and regression in the acquisition of skills. The language skills of the slow learner are not age appropriate, but the language skills of the learning disabled student often are.

Behavior is another area in which the teacher can identify the difference between a slow learner and a student with a learning disability. The slow learner shows little understanding of the consequences of immature behavior, in direct contrast to a student with a learning disability, who may be acting inappropriately but is fully aware of the consequences of misbehavior. Unfortunately, this understanding may not guide his or her behavior.

Even with intervention, the slow learner's progress will be very slow. When intervention techniques are used with a student who has a learning disability, there may be steady and near-normal progression in academics in some cases.

Strategies for Educators

The student with a learning disability may exhibit one or more of the other disabilities covered in this book. The teacher needs to know what the student's specific disabilities are. Only then can the educational needs of the student be met. For example, if the student has a visual processing dysfunction, it would be counterproductive to teach in the visual mode. The teacher should know what the student's learning modality is in order to exploit the student's strengths. However, a multisensory approach is best if the needs of all students in the class are to be met.

The student with a learning disability requires a well-structured environment. Students generally are able to accomplish more when the teacher routinely outlines the day's activities on the chalkboard and sets goals for the day. Reviewing the schedule and the rules before a new activity also helps the student with a learning disability bridge the transition from one activity to another.

Some students with learning disabilities are easily overstimulated by certain classroom activities or excessive talking. This often leads to misbehavior by the student that may be disruptive to the class. It is the teacher's responsibility to help the student regain composure. A teacher can provide a "time-out" place in the classroom where the student can be away from the ongoing activity. Or a teacher can send the student on an errand or to the school library. At no time should this be used as a punitive action but merely as an opportunity to provide a quiet time for the student.

The learning modality of many students with learning disabilities is kinesthetic. These students learn best when they can see and touch concrete objects relating to the subject being taught. They also get a kinesthetic image if they form the letters or numbers with their fingers in the air. Depending on the age of the student, the use of sand and sandpaper to form letters or numbers produces the same effect. However, in the regular class, this type of kinesthetic mode will set the student apart from the rest of the class unless all are using the same method. The use of manipulatives for the entire class or a small group of students is less intimidating, and everyone in the class will benefit.

The teacher needs to be flexible in assignment requirements. When a student has difficulty writing a report, the teacher should consider accepting oral or taped reports. Computers are extremely helpful to students who have difficulty writing reports, and many types of software are available to help make writing easier. It may be necessary to reduce the length of the written assignments so that the student with a learning disability can successfully complete the task.

Above all, the teacher should recognize the successes—no matter how small—of students who are learning disabled. As with all students, there should be immediate and positive feedback. Behavior modification techniques may also foster the student's desire to achieve.

It is essential to diagnose learning disabilities and related problems as early as possible. Without recognition and help, students become increasingly frustrated and distressed by persistent failure. By the time they reach high school, they may quit trying. However, children whose problems are recognized early and treated appropriately can develop strategies to compensate for their disabilities and lead successful and rewarding lives.

Mental Retardation

Definition

In 1992, the American Association on Mental Retardation defined mental retardation according to three criteria: intellectual functioning level below a 70 to 75 IQ, significant limitations existing in two or more adaptive skill areas, and the presence of these conditions since childhood (Luckasson et al., 1992).

Background

The Association for Retarded Citizens states that more than 100,000 newborn children are likely to be mentally retarded. It is estimated that 1 out of every 10 families has a member who is mentally retarded. According to the 1990 census, there are approximately 6.2 million to 7.5 million people who have mental retardation (Batshaw, 1991).

The President's Committee on Mental Retardation states that 75% of the mentally retarded population comes from urban and rural poverty areas. Causative factors may be the result of malnutrition, disease, lead poisoning, and inadequate medical care in those areas. An additional cause may be under-stimulation of the child after birth. A child has a basic need for everyday, enriching experiences, and a lack of them can curtail his or her mental development. Mental retardation can occur in any family, regardless of racial, educational, or social background.

Mental retardation can be classified as mild, moderate, severe, or profound. The American Association on Mental Retardation, however, no longer labels individuals according to these categories but looks instead at the intensity and pattern of changing supports needed by the individual during his or her lifetime.

Eighty-seven percent of those with mental retardation will be mildly affected and only a little slower than average in learning new information, whereas 13% will have serious limitations in functioning.

Persons who are mildly affected differ primarily in their rate and degree of mental development. In some of those cases, retardation may not become apparent until the child enters school. In others, it may become obvious well before the child is of school age.

Severely and profoundly retarded people account for 5% of those with mental retardation (Association for Retarded Citizens, 1987). In addition to intellectual impairment, they frequently have other disabilities, such as cerebral palsy, epilepsy or a similar seizure disorder, or visual or hearing impairments. Although they will receive special training, they may be dependent on others for the rest of their lives. The educator's primary goal for the profoundly retarded is to help them develop skills that will enable them to care for their own personal needs and work in a sheltered workplace or home environment.

Most cases of severe retardation can be attributed to genetic irregularities or chromosomal abnormalities. Down syndrome and other inherited or congenital conditions account for many cases of mental retardation in children. Mental retardation may also result from birth trauma or infection at birth or in early childhood. Biological factors may include asphyxia, blood incompatibilities between the pregnant woman and fetus, and maternal infections. Certain drugs have also been linked to problems in fetal development that result in mental retardation.

Although mental retardation is permanent and irreversible, there are authorities who believe that 50% of the cases could be prevented. Routine screening and immunization of the pregnant woman before transfusions, pregnancy, and childbirth would help prevent the type of mental retardation caused by Rh hemolytic blood disease. An infant affected during gestation by Rh factor incompatibility should have a blood exchange at the time of birth.

Children between the ages of 18 months and 24 months should be immunized for *Hemophilus influenza* to prevent mental retardation caused by bacterial meningitis. In addition, all preschool children should be tested for the presence of lead in their bodies. If the level is dangerously high, treatment should follow, and sources of lead poisoning should be identified and removed from the child's environment.

Because the developmental rate may be much slower for children who are mentally retarded, it is important to begin appropriate educational services in infancy and to continue throughout the developmental period.

Characteristics

Short-term memory impairment is common among children with mental retardation. Because of this deficit, it takes much longer for those children to learn a skill. Continuous repetition is needed, as they may have difficulty remembering what they learned the previous day. Children with mental retardation are often unable to form generalizations from their learning experiences and thus may have trouble applying what they learn to life situations.

Most children who are mentally retarded exhibit the social behavior of a younger child and prefer playing with younger children. Their emotions are usually inappropriate for a particular situation and generally expressed in a childlike manner. Their language and speech skills may be well below those of their peers, and they may have difficulty using complex language and following complex directions.

Individuals with mental retardation will develop their academic, social, and vocational skills differently, depending on whether the impairment is mild, moderate, severe, or profound. Their less-developed intellectual ability and social skills may lead to rejection by others and a lowering of their self-esteem. However, it is possible for many who are retarded to have normal life patterns.

Strategies for Educators

Many regular classrooms have students who are mentally retarded—generally mildly to moderately retarded. The teacher should set realistic goals for students with mental retardation because it is paramount that they feel successful in their endeavors.

Tasks that many people learn to do without instruction are difficult for the student who is mentally retarded. The use of manipulatives and concrete objects is necessary. Teachers also need to break tasks down into smaller steps or segments, with each step being carefully taught and retaught. Peer tutoring, in particular, is very effective in reinforcing the concept to be learned.

A learning center with high-interest activities in a designated area of the room can also be very helpful for the student. The learning center can be designed to focus on a particular need for all students and as a place where students can complete assignments at their own pace.

The teacher should require less written work from a mentally retarded student. If beneficial, the student should be allowed to tape-record the "written" assignment for replay when needed.

The mentally retarded need to be taught tasks that help them develop working skills they can use in real-life situations. Students who are mentally retarded should be given checklists to account for homework or for completed, turned-in assignments. Many tasks in the school library as well as the office can be successfully handled by mentally retarded students.

In today's society, the trend is for persons who are mentally retarded to work in a supportive environment in the general sector. Many jobs in the workplace, such as restaurant work and assembly production lines, consist of repetitive tasks. Being able to enter the mainstream gives those who are mentally retarded feelings of success and accomplishment and allows them to become productive and full participants in our society.

Muscular Dystrophy

Definition

Muscular dystrophy is the general designation for a group of chronic, hereditary diseases that consist of slow, progressive wasting and weakening of the muscles.

Background

Muscular dystrophy should not be confused with multiple sclerosis, which is an acquired disease and usually starts in early adult life. Unlike multiple sclerosis, muscular dystrophy is an inherited muscular disorder affecting children.

It is estimated that 200,000 Americans of all ages are affected by muscular dystrophy. There are several types of muscular dystrophy: facioscapulohumeral muscular dystrophy, limb-girdle muscular dystrophy, myotonic dystrophy, ocular dystrophy, Duchenne muscular dystrophy, and Becker's muscular dystrophy.

Facioscapulohumeral muscular dystrophy, which usually appears between the ages of 10 and 40, affects the muscles of the upper arms, shoulder girdle, and face. Progression is slow and rarely leads to complete disability.

Limb-girdle muscular dystrophy differs from facioscapulohumeral muscular dystrophy in its lack of involvement of the facial muscles; it mainly affects the muscles of the hips and shoulders. Limb-girdle dystrophy usually starts in late childhood or the early 20s. As in facioscapulohumeral muscular dystrophy, the progression of this form of dystrophy is slow.

Myotonic dystrophy is a relatively rare form of dystrophy that affects the hands and feet. Muscles are unable to relax for several seconds after a forceful contraction. Infants show a pronounced floppiness and are slow to develop.

Ocular dystrophy is another rare form. This type affects the eyes and throat. It can result in double vision, drooping eyelids, and difficulty swallowing because of degeneration of the throat muscles.

Duchenne muscular dystrophy is the most common form, and it appears only in males. About 1 to 2 in 10,000 boys are affected, and approximately one third of those are mentally retarded. This type of dystrophy is genetic, inherited through a recessive sex-linked gene affecting boys, but it may also be passed on to a female, who then becomes a carrier. A female carrier has a 50% chance of passing on this disease to her infant son, and her daughter has a 50% chance of becoming a carrier.

The symptoms of Duchenne muscular dystrophy appear within the first 3 years of life. The first muscles to weaken are the hip-girdle muscles followed by a weakening of the shoulder muscles. There can be an uncertain gait, frequent falling, and difficulty getting up from the floor or climbing stairs. By the time a boy reaches age 12, he usually must use a wheelchair. A steady weakening of the respiratory muscles makes it hard to breathe. The heart muscle is also weakened, and this often leads to heart failure. Duchenne muscular dystrophy progresses steadily and most who have this disease do not live beyond age 20.

The symptoms of *Becker's muscular dystrophy* are similar to those of Duchenne muscular dystrophy. There may also be curvature of the spine, and the muscles may appear bulky because when the muscles waste away they are replaced with fat. This type of dystrophy starts later in childhood and progression is slow.

At present, medical intervention can neither cure nor halt the disease.

Characteristics

The physical characteristics of individuals with muscular dystrophy have been briefly stated above under the various types of dystrophy. These individuals require assistance with their personal hygiene, eating, and dressing. This dependence on others understandably affects the individual with muscular dystrophy, and, as with any other severe physical disability, there can be many psychological and social problems as well.

Strategies for Educators

Although many students with muscular dystrophy have learned to adapt to their environment, the teacher can help create a classroom environment to meet their specific educational and physical needs. Although technological aids are available that are useful to students with muscular dystrophy, these devices may create conditions of which teachers need to be aware.

If a student is in a wheelchair or is using other assistance devices, physical movement can be very burdensome. Extra time should be allowed for the student when he or she has to move from one place to another. Depending on the particular situation, another student can provide help in the transition. It must be remembered, however, that many do not want or need this additional help, and the student's wishes should be respected. Students wish to achieve, but also wish to be as independent as possible.

Cooperative learning is an excellent experience for most students with muscular dystrophy. Teaming together with peers provides an opportunity to interact with others, make new friends, be accepted by others, and work cooperatively. Establishing a network of friends is important to the student with a disability, and this network may continue to grow and extend beyond the school environment.

Students with muscular dystrophy should remain active as long as possible in order to keep their healthy muscles in good condition. Short-term rehabilitation efforts can be beneficial in the early stages of the disorder, but not in the later stages. Educators should encourage independence to avoid self-esteem problems associated with dependence on others. For successful rehabilitation, normal social opportunities should be encouraged whenever possible.

Counseling can be beneficial for both the student and family members. Many psychological problems resulting from the disability can be overcome. Counseling also helps family members by easing the burden of dealing with muscular dystrophy on their own.

Speech Disorders

Definition

Speech is considered to be impaired "when it deviates so far from the speech of other people that it calls attention to itself, interferes with communication, or causes the speaker or [the speaker's] listeners to be distressed" (Van Ripper, 1978, p. 43).

Background

Communication disorders encompass both language and speech deficits. However, an individual with speech problems has difficulty only with communication skills, whereas a person with a language disorder has difficulty not only with the expression of ideas but also with the reception of language. Speech problems are more prevalent than language problems. The U.S. Department of Health and Human Services estimates that speech disorders affect 10% to 15% of preschoolers and about 6% of children in grades 1 through 12. It is also estimated that there are 5 million to 10 million children in the United States who need speech training. Ten of every 100 children can be expected to have a speech disorder (National Information Center for Children and Youth with Disabilities, 1990c).

Speech centers are located in the left hemisphere of the brain. However, researchers have found that there is a degree of bilateralism between the left and right hemispheres. Any damage to the brain can lead to a speech disorder. Communication disorders such as autism, cerebral palsy, mental retardation, hearing impairment, and aphasia, which have an organic or physical origin, are treated under separate headings.

The four basic components of speech are *articulation, phonation, resonance,* and *rhythm.* Articulation refers to the ability to make specific sounds, and phonation is the actual utterance of words. Resonance is the reinforcement and prolongation of sounds by vibrations. The rate and timing of speech is the rhythm with which it is spoken.

Speech disorders are common in most children who have or have had a cleft lip or palate. A cleft lip is characterized by the separation of the two sides of the lip. It often includes a cleft in the back of the upper jaw and upper gum. A cleft palate is characterized by an opening in the roof of the mouth from behind the teeth to the nasal cavity, and its severity can vary from child to child.

Both a cleft lip and a cleft palate can be present at birth. In 1989, the American Medical Association stated that of every nine babies affected, two have only a cleft lip, three have only a cleft palate, and four have both. According to the Cleft Palate Foundation, 1 out of every 700 to 750 babies is born with a cleft lip, a cleft palate, or both (Lynch, 1989). Because clefts tend to run in families, heredity appears to be a factor.

Children born with clefts often experience problems with articulation and resonance, and their speech development is slower than that of other children. They may also have missing, malformed, or malpositioned teeth that require medical attention. Ear infections, which may lead to hearing loss along with accompanying speech disorders, are also common among these children.

Fortunately, with new surgical procedures, a cleft lip can be repaired when a baby is 3 months old, and a cleft palate can be repaired before a baby is 1 year old. In addition to corrective surgery, the medical profession has also designed appliances to replace the missing palate. With early intervention by medical professionals and therapists, most children are able to compensate for or overcome their speech disorders.

Stuttering, or stammering, is another kind of speech disorder. Generally, stuttering in children starts before age 8, and 75% stop stuttering by the time they reach adolescence. It has been estimated that 2.5 million Americans stutter and that five times more men than women stutter.

Although the exact cause of stuttering is unknown, the tendency to stutter runs in families. Some researchers believe it might be the result of a subtle brain damage. Others feel that stuttering is primarily a psychological problem. Stuttering can often be improved by the use of speech therapy or electronic aids, or both.

Characteristics

Many children with speech disorders have characteristics that are common to other children. However, the student with a speech disability often has difficulty combining speech sounds for communication. This leads the person to self-correct and hesitate when trying to convey his or her thoughts.

Articulation problems are common in individuals with speech disorders. Some sounds may be completely omitted during speech, so that instead of saying "I see a bike" a child might say "I ee a ike." Some students with articulation problems may have difficulty pronouncing the letters *l* or *t*, or they may substitute one sound for another. The National Institute of Health uses the cartoon character Elmer Fudd as an example of someone with an articulation disorder when he talks about the "scwewy wabbit." To accurately repeat a sound, a child must be able to perceive its unique characteristics. Although many speech patterns may be called "baby talk" and be part of a young child's normal development, they can become problems if they are not outgrown.

Students who stutter generally have prolonged speech sounds, repeated hesitation, and a delayed utterance of words. Under stress, their vocal cords go into spasms prior to speaking. To relax the vocal cords and keep them open, stutterers can prolong their inhalations and exhalations before speaking. Even though a person might stutter while speaking, he or she will usually have no difficulty singing.

A lack of communication skills may lead to intense feelings of frustration, isolation, discouragement, and possible outbursts of anger. Many children who have severe speech disorders and physical impairments have to contend with not only their speech but other physical disabilities as well.

Strategies for Educators

Because stuttering is the most obvious form of speech disorder that students recognize, the teacher needs to explain to them what stuttering is. It is also helpful to discuss the lives of the many successful people who have overcome their own stuttering. The teacher can read stories about these people to younger students, and assign to older students oral and written reports concerning successful people with the disability. The following is a partial list of people who overcame their stuttering problems: Moses, Hebrew prophet; Sir Isaac Newton, English mathematician and natural philosopher; Marilyn Monroe, actress; Winston Churchill, prime minister of Great Britain during World War II; Kim Philby, British spy; Raymond Massey, actor; James Earl Jones, actor; Ben Johnson, Olympic runner; Greg Louganis, Olympic diver; Carly Simon, singer; Dave Taylor, former hockey star with the Los Angeles Kings; Lester Hayes, former defensive back with the Oakland and L.A. Raiders; Bo Jackson, football and baseball star; Jimmy Stewart, actor; Peggy Lipton, actress; John "Scatman" Larkin, jazz musician; Bill Walton, former basketball player and current TV commentator; and Mel Tillis, country-western singer.

The teacher should serve as a role model for students and never criticize a student's speech. A student who stutters needs to feel relaxed and comfortable in his or her classroom without fear of ridicule.

The Stuttering Foundation of America suggests that a teacher should allow time for the student to adjust to the class. During this time, questions should be asked that only require a few words to respond. When everyone in the class is going to be asked a question, the student who stutters should be questioned early. The longer the wait, the more the student's tension will increase as he or she waits for a turn. Everyone in the class, not just the student who stutters, should be allowed as much time as they need to answer questions. It is better for all students to think through their answers rather than respond quickly with little thought given to the question.

Reading aloud in the class can be very threatening for a student who stutters. But if the teacher has the entire class read in unison, the student is not made to feel different and can experience fluency and satisfaction. In time, he or she may feel more competent and able to read without this backup. In some cases, the student can be given the reading material to practice reading at home.

The teacher should discourage and, whenever possible, prevent teasing in the classroom on the part of the nondisabled students. It is very painful for a student who stutters to be teased. If teasing occurs, the teacher should talk privately to the student who was teased and let him or her know that you take such behavior seriously and will take steps to correct it. The teacher should also tell the student that most children are teased for many different things at one time or another. It is helpful if the teacher shares personal experiences about being teased. The teacher should also have a private talk with the offending students. Explain to them that the speech disorder is very distressing to the student who stutters, and that teasing can exacerbate the stuttering. To help them understand the effects of teasing on an individual, the teacher should focus on the feelings the students had when other students teased them. Punishment should be avoided as it only intensifies the students' negative feelings about the student who stutters and makes the situation worse. The majority of students want the teacher's approval and, if asked in private, will not only empathize with the student who stutters but stop teasing their classmate.

Acceptance by his or her peers is essential to the student who stutters. Cooperative learning projects can provide this opportunity. The teacher can also select an understanding and caring person to be the learning "buddy"—someone who can be a special friend to the student who stutters.

A child with a speech disorder needs motivation to communicate, and in order to communicate successfully, a stimulating and supportive environment is mandatory. Criticism does not help a student overcome a speech disorder. When a child who has a speech disorder has difficulty communicating, others may attempt to hasten the child's speech. This should always be avoided. Patience and consideration are necessary for all students who have a speech disorder.

Spina Bifida

Definition

Spina bifida is a congenital defect in which part of one or more vertebrae fails to develop completely, leaving part of the spinal cord exposed. According to the Spina Bifida Association of America (n.d.a), "It is a defect in the bony spinal column where the spine failed to close up to form one piece during the first two months of pregnancy."

Background

Spina bifida is a permanently disabling defect that affects newborns. It occurs with a higher frequency than muscular dystrophy, polio, and cystic fibrosis combined. At this time, its exact cause is unknown. It is believed that both genetic and nongenetic factors may be involved. The occurrence in siblings is approximately 3% to 5%. If a woman already has a child with spina bifida, she is 10 times more likely than average to have another affected child. The incidence increases in the pregnancies of both very young women and older women.

There are four types of spina bifida: *spina bifida occulta, myelocele, meningocele,* and *encephalocele.*

Spina bifida occulta is the most common and least serious form of spina bifida. In spina bifida occulta, there is an opening in one or more of the vertebrae of the spinal column without apparent damage to the spinal cord. There is little external evidence of this form except for a possible dimple or tuft of hair over the underlying abnormality. At least 40% of all Americans may have spina bifida occulta. Most do not even know they have it, because they experience few or no symptoms. This type often goes completely unnoticed in children.

Myelocele, also known as *meningomyelocele,* is the severest form of spina bifida. A portion of the spinal cord protrudes through the back. In some cases the sacs are covered with skin and in others, tissues and nerves are exposed. A child with myelocele is generally severely handicapped and may have other associated abnormalities such as cerebral palsy, epilepsy, mental retardation, and visual problems.

Approximately 70% to 90% of children born with myelocele also have hydrocephalus. Although this condition can occur without spina bifida, the two conditions often occur together. In hydrocephalus, there is a fluid buildup in the brain. This can be controlled by a surgical procedure called *shunting*. If a shunt is not implanted, pressure builds up and may cause seizures, brain damage, or blindness.

Meningocele is less severe than myelocele. The spinal cord remains intact but the meninges, or protective coverings around the spinal cord, have pushed out through the opening in a sac called meningocele. This form can be repaired with little or no damage to the nerve pathways.

Encephalocele is a rare type of spina bifida. In this type, the protrusion occurs through the skull and results in severe brain damage.

Twenty years ago, 90% of infants with spina bifida died, but because of advances in medical technology, infants born with this birth defect are now expected to have a normal life span. Because there is no central registry for persons affected by this birth defect, the exact number cannot be accurately stated. However, the Spina Bifida Association is currently working on compiling such a registry.

Characteristics

Depending on the type of spina bifida a child has, he or she may be heavily braced or be indistinguishable from other children. According to the Spina Bifida Association of America (n.d.b), the following general characteristics may be present in students with spina bifida:

- Varying degrees of paralysis
- Weakness in the feet, ankles, and/or legs
- Diminished feeling in the feet, ankles, and/or legs
- Incontinence of both bowel and bladder from nerve damage, resulting in occasional accidents and a probable need for clean intermittent catheterization during school hours
- Shunting of fluid from the brain
- Learning disabilities, perhaps resulting from perceptual difficulties and/or damage to the brain
- Motor difficulties in the arms and hands, with perhaps some slowness in performing certain tasks
- Possible absence seizures, such as staring into space momentarily, or motor involvement ranging from tremors to spasms of the large muscles

Children with spina bifida are similar to other children in their intellectual ability, ranging from gifted to developmentally delayed. The majority will have normal to above-normal intelligence.

Strategies for Educators

Inclusion of a child with spina bifida with students without disabilities—where they are provided a school pattern that is as nearly normal as possible—is of great value. In some cases, certain changes may have to be made for the school to accommodate the student with spina bifida. Depending on the particular type of spina bifida, special architectural adaptations may need to be made, such as adding elevators or ramps. Special equipment, such as wheelchairs, crutches, or braces, may also be needed.

Some students with spina bifida may have secondary disabilities, such as seizures, cerebral palsy, learning disabilities, or other disabling conditions. Suggestions for those disabilities are included in other sections of this book.

The teacher needs to set realistic goals for students that will encourage and increase their desire to achieve. Students' strengths should be emphasized and opportunities provided to demonstrate their talents in ways that allow them to be successful and gain the approval of their peers.

Comments and responses to the student should always be phrased in a positive manner. Focusing on the student's abilities and positive aspects of his or her personality will strengthen the student's feeling of confidence and self-worth.

The teacher should help the other students in the class recognize the similarities among all students and realize that students with spina bifida are more like them than they are different from them.

Spinal Cord Injury

Definition

A spinal cord injury is caused by trauma to the 18-inch cylinder of nerve tissue running down the central canal of the spine that damages the nerve fibers.

Background

The spinal cord and the brain constitute the central nervous system, which controls all human performance and behavior. The spinal cord carries messages from the brain to the internal organs, muscles, and skin. These messages inform the body what to do or what to ignore. In turn, messages are sent back to the brain about what is happening to the body—for example, sensations of heat or cold. When the spinal cord is damaged there is no communication between the brain and the spinal cord, resulting in loss of sensation, muscle weakness, or paralysis. The degree of severity may be mild, serious, or fatal.

According to the National Institute of Health and Human Development (1981), the higher on the spine the injury, the greater the disability. When injury occurs at the neck level, both the arms and legs may be paralyzed. This type of paralysis is referred to as *quadriplegia* or *tetraplegia*. According to the Rehabilitation Learning Center at

Harborview Medical Center (1995) in Seattle, Washington, the term *tetraplegia* is preferred.

If an individual has an injury at the chest level, the arms are spared but the legs and lower part of the body are affected. This is generally referred to as *paraplegia* and the individual is considered to be paraplegic. Many use the term *paraplegic* when referring to anyone who has a paralysis.

The American Medical Association identifies three basic types of force that cause spinal cord injury: longitudinal compression, hinging, and shearing. In longitudinal compression, the vertebrae are crushed, often from a fall. When the spinal column receives extreme bending movement, for example, from a whiplash injury, it is called hinging. Shearing is a combination of both hinging and a twisting motion, generally caused by an individual's being hit by a motor vehicle.

In 1994, it was estimated that 500,000 Americans suffered from spinal cord injuries, and an additional 12,000 to 15,000 individuals sustain spinal cord injuries each year. The majority of people average 19 years of age at the time of spinal cord injury. The primary causes of spinal cord injury include but are not limited to falls, automobile accidents, sports accidents, gunshot wounds, and other acts of violence.

The American Paralysis Association states that in the first few hours after an injury, the spinal cord begins to "self-destruct" (National Institute of Health and Human Development, 1981). The injury sets off a series of self-destructive cellular occurrences. Swelling, hemorrhaging, and a drop in blood pressure that lowers the blood supply to the injured spinal cord occur. The nerve cells die, leaving a gap in the spinal cord; scar tissue forms, which destroys the connections in the cord; and paralysis sets in.

Until recently, paralysis was considered incurable. Now, because of ongoing, extensive research, there is hope. Areas of research include therapeutic and pharmacological approaches, transplantation to prevent the degeneration of the spinal cord, and the use of natural substances to promote neuronal growth. Much of the research is focused on neural regeneration and recovery for the patient who has a spinal cord injury.

Characteristics

Characteristics of spinal cord injury may include loss of sensation, muscle weakness, loss of bladder and bowel control, and paralysis.

Some students with a spinal cord injury will have neuromuscular degeneration as well as other disabilities, such as spina bifida, cerebral palsy, or muscular dystrophy.

To suddenly find oneself paralyzed presents many difficulties, and significant psychological and emotional problems may occur in attempting to adjust to the paralysis. Each case of spinal cord injury is different, and the inner strength an individual has to surmount the numerous problems associated with a spinal cord injury varies.

Strategies for Educators

The classroom teacher can expect that some, but not all, students with spinal cord injury will exhibit immature behavior. Although some may manifest intellectual impairment, others will have a similar degree of intellectual ability as other students.

Because of impaired health, the student with a spinal cord injury may often be absent, and assignments should be adjusted as needed. The teacher should also provide the parent, as well as the support personnel, with the assigned work. This will help the student keep up with academic goals.

As with other disabilities, the teacher needs to confer with the other professionals involved with the student. Special arrangements must be made to accommodate the physical needs of the student. Depending on the severity of the injury to the spinal cord, assistance devices, such as a wheelchair, tilt table, and so forth may be needed.

The teacher should make use of the many electronic aids that are currently available, such as computers and tape recorders, to provide educational support for the student. Communications technology has also developed many new devices for students with severe disabilities; for example, software is available for computers that allows a student who is unable to hold a book to read the text on the computer screen. A page of text appears on the screen, and the student uses a customized chin switch to enter the commands.

Fortunately, the new advances in technology aids enable individuals with spinal cord injuries to have more mobility and be able to achieve greater independence. Continued research may one day find a cure for this once-incurable condition.

In *Spinal Cord Injury* (National Institute of Health and Human Development, 1981), Howard A. Rusk, one of the world's best-known rehabilitation specialists, is quoted as follows:

Great ceramics are not made by putting clay in the sun; they come only from the white heat of the kiln. In the firing process, some pieces are broken, but those that survive the heat are transformed from clay into porcelain and are objects of art, and so it is with people.

Those who, through medical skill, opportunity, work and courage, survive their illness or overcome their handicap and take their places back in the world have a depth of spirit that you and I can hardly measure. They haven't wasted their pain. (p. 28)

Tourette Syndrome

Definition

According to the Tourette Syndrome Association (1994), *Tourette syndrome* (TS) is a neurological disorder characterized by tics. The American Psychiatric Association defines a *tic* as "an 'involuntary,' sudden, rapid, recurrent, nonrhythmic, stereotyped motor movement or vocalization. It is experienced as irresistible, but can be suppressed for varying lengths of time" (Comings, 1990, p. 12).

Background

In 1825, there was one reported case in medical literature of a woman who had all the symptoms of TS. The disorder was named after Gilles de la Tourette, a French neurologist, who in 1885 described it as involving muscle tics, vocal noises, and compulsive swearing. He also noted that the tics were usually of short duration and intermittent, in direct contrast to other similar disorders.

The Tourette Syndrome Association states that there may be as many as 2 million people with the disorder who have not been diagnosed as having TS. The official estimate of the National Institutes of Health is that 100,000 Americans have diagnosed, full-blown TS (Ottinger & Gaffney, 1995).

Although its exact cause is unknown, researchers believe that TS may be caused by a chemical imbalance in the brain that is the result of an abnormality in the neurotransmitters, the chemicals that carry signals between nerve cells. Current research indicates that the abnormal metabolism of one of the neurotransmitters (dopamine) and serotonin is involved.

Three times as many males than females have TS, and it is believed that TS is inherited. A person who has a dominant gene carrying the symptoms of TS has a 50% chance of passing the gene on to his or her children. The gene-carrying child of a person with TS is three to four times more likely to be a son than a daughter. Children of parents who have TS also have a higher incidence of developing obsessive-compulsive behaviors. In cases where TS is not inherited, the cause remains unknown.

Tourette syndrome is not a degenerative disease. It can begin abruptly with multiple symptoms involving movements and sounds. These symptoms can disappear for months and weeks at a time. A remission sometimes occurs after adolescence, but TS is generally a lifelong, chronic condition. Individuals with TS can live a normal life span.

At present, no blood analysis or other type of neurological testing exists to diagnose TS. The medical profession may order tests to rule out other possible ailments before a diagnosis of TS is made. TS is difficult to diagnose simply by observing behavior because tics are unpredictable and often change in frequency and type. Rating scales and questionnaires are used along with the observable symptoms in the diagnosis. A diagnosis of TS requires the individual to have had both vocal and motor tics for more than a year that either change in severity or increase in duration. The American Psychiatric Association (1994) uses the following criteria for diagnosing Tourette syndrome:

A. Both multiple motor and one or more vocal tics have been present at some time during the illness, although not necessarily concurrently. (A tic is a sudden, rapid, recurrent, non-rhythmic, stereotyped motor movement or vocalization.)

B. The tics occur many times a day (usually in bouts), nearly every day or intermittently throughout a period of more than 1 year, and during this period there was never a tic-free period of more than 3 consecutive months.

C. The disturbance causes marked distress or significant impairment in social, occupational, or other important areas of functioning.

D. The onset is before age of 18 years.

E. The disturbance is not due to the direct physiological effects of a substance (e.g., stimulants) or a general medical condition (e.g., Huntington's disease or postviral encephalitis). (p. 103)

The tics and behavioral symptoms in the majority of TS cases do not hinder the individual. If the symptoms interfere with normal functioning, medications are sometimes prescribed. There are some behavior therapies that help the individual to substitute one tic for another that is more acceptable. The disorder is not psychological, but some individuals develop emotional problems trying to deal with the symptoms of TS. Psychotherapy may help the individual and his or her family cope with the problems associated with TS.

When a child is diagnosed as having TS, it is important to start treatment early because many of the manifestations of the syndrome are considered bizarre and disruptive, and the child may be excluded from many activities and normal interpersonal relationships. At this time, there is no cure for TS.

Characteristics

Tics are categorized as either *motor* or *vocal* and *simple* or *complex*. The Neuropsychiatric Movement Disorder Staff at the University of Iowa Hospitals and Clinics listed the following characteristics for motor and vocal tics:

- Simple motor tics: eye blinking, eye rolling, squinting, head jerking, facial grimacing, nose twitching, lip smacking, tongue thrusting, mouth opening, leg jerking, arm flexing, or flappings
- Complex motor tics: hitting self or others, jumping, touching self or others, smelling hands or objects, clapping, pinching, touching objects (haphemania), stooping, hopping, kicking, throwing, squatting, skipping, somersaulting, stepping backwards, deep knee bending, foot tapping, foot shaking, foot dragging, chewing on clothes, scratching, kissing self or others, pulling at clothes, or any other combinations of movements done repeatedly
- Simple vocal tics: throat clearing, grunts, sniffs, snorts, squeaking, coughs, humming, screams, spitting, puffing, whistling, honking, stammering or stuttering, hissing, laughing, shouts, barking, moaning, guttural sounds, noisy breathing, gasping, gurgling, squeaking, clicking or clacking, hiccups, 'tsk' and 'pft' noises

- Complex vocal tics: any understandable words or phrases (may include echoing) (Ottinger & Gaffney, 1995)

Other associated characteristics of TS, which may or may not be present in all cases, are

- Repeating the speech of others (echolalia)
- Repeating their own words (palilalia)
- Involuntary utterances of obscenities or socially taboo phrases (coprolalia)
- Making obscene gestures (copropraxia)

TS individuals may exhibit obsessive-compulsive behaviors—for example, continually washing their hands until they become raw or touching something a certain number of times. Self-touching is very common among TS individuals.

Individuals with TS have the same range of intellectual functioning as the general population. Some individuals with TS may also have other disabilities such as emotional disturbances, ADHD, dyslexia, aphasia, autism, or learning disabilities. Strategies for students with these disabilities can also be useful for students with TS.

Strategies for Educators

Having a student with TS in the class can be very disturbing to the teacher who is unprepared. Because the acts of a TS student are involuntary, patience and consideration for the student are required on the part of the teacher. Most students with TS can sense when their tics are about to precede a severe outburst and know when they need to leave the classroom. The teacher should preselect a secluded area where a TS student can go before a severe attack begins.

A student with TS should be given opportunities to take occasional short breaks from the classroom routine in order to release tics. For example, the teacher might send the student on errands to the office or the library to give the student time to regain his or her composure. Often, just allowing the student to leave the room voluntarily for a drink of water is sufficient. Short breaks between activities also give the student time to relieve inner stress.

When giving long-term assignments, the teacher should make certain the student knows well in advance what is expected and when the assignment is due. This will ease the stress experienced when the TS student is required to complete an assignment in a short period of time. Timed tests can be especially stressful for a TS student and can increase the possibility of severe tics. It is always better to allow students to work at their own pace. Using tape recorders, typewriters, and computers can also eliminate some of the classroom stress for the TS student.

Because a TS student is likely to have a very poor self-image, the teacher needs to be accepting and positive in all dealings with the student. If the student's conduct is not disruptive, the teacher should ignore the behavior. However, a teacher's intervention can often help a student with a compulsive behavior. For example, if the student continually taps a pencil on the desk, the teacher might provide the student with a small piece of foam on which to tap the pencil. Without the knowledge of the others in the class, the teacher and student should develop a special signal so that the student will know when his or her behavior is inappropriate. Above all, the teacher should not allow the student with TS to use his or her symptoms as a means of control.

Transition times can be occasions for many confrontations among the students in any class. To avoid unnecessary conflict, the student with TS should be allowed to leave a few minutes before the class ends. A younger student with TS should be next to the teacher at the front of the line when leaving the classroom.

Given that TS is a lifelong condition, students without TS often wonder if anyone with TS could be successful in life. The following is a partial list of people with TS: Samuel Johnson, author of the English dictionary; André Malroux, French author; Jim Eisenreich, Philadelphia Phillies outfielder; Lowell Handler, photojournalist; Desirée Ledet, actress; Mohamoud Abdul Rauf (formerly Chris Jackson), Denver Nuggets basketball player; Laurel Chiten, filmmaker, producer, and director; and Shane Fistel, Toronto artist.

Medical research may eventually find a way to prevent Tourette syndrome's being transmitted from one generation to the next. With better understanding and treatment, many individuals with TS now lead very productive and successful lives.

Visual Impairment

Definition

Visual impairment is the diminishment of the ability to see. The terms *partially sighted, legally blind, low vision,* and *totally blind* are commonly used to describe visual impairments.

Background

It is estimated that more than 40 million people in the world are either totally blind or partially sighted. There are 530,000 legally blind people in the United States, and 47,000 new cases are reported each year. The vast majority of cases occur in people age 65 and older.

There is a widespread misconception that blindness equals total blackness. This is not true. Both the eye and the brain are involved with vision, and there are many degrees of visual impairment.

A person who is *partially sighted* has lost most of his or her sight, cannot see much more than light or some large shapes, and has central visual acuity of 20/70 to 20/200 in the better eye with correction. A partially sighted person with correction sees at 20 feet what the normal eye sees at 70 to 200 feet.

A person who is *legally blind* has central visual acuity of 20/200 or less with correction in the better eye or has a very limited field of vision, such as 20 degrees at its widest point. This means that even with correction, there is no more than 10% normal vision in the better eye and the field of vision is no greater than 20 degrees. A person who is legally blind sees with correction at 20 feet what the normal eye sees from a distance of 200 or more feet.

The term *low vision* usually refers to a severe visual impairment, but it is not necessarily limited to distant vision. Low vision also applies to all who have difficulty reading newspapers or other reading material, even with correction.

There are many causes of impaired vision. It can result from degeneration of the eyeball, or the optic nerve or nerve pathways connecting the eye to the brain may be impaired, causing loss of vision. Damage to the brain can also cause vision problems. Blindness is often the result of injury or disease. No one is immune from developing a vision disorder.

Some vision disorders are refractive errors that can usually be corrected with proper lenses. Refractive errors include hyperopia, myopia, and astigmatism.

Hyperopia, also called *farsightedness*, is a condition in which light rays focus behind the retina. Vision is better for distant objects than for near objects, which are blurred and unclear. A convex corrective lens before the eye increases the bending of the light rays, thereby aiding in focusing.

Myopia is also referred to as *nearsightedness*. In this case, the light rays are focused in front of the retina. Vision is better for near objects than for far objects, which are blurred. A concave corrective lens refocuses the image on the retina.

Astigmatism results from an irregularity in the curvature of the cornea or lens of the eye. This curvature causes light rays to be refracted unevenly at different planes so that horizontal and vertical rays are focused at two different places on the retina, resulting in blurred or imperfect vision. Astigmatism generally can be corrected with proper lenses.

Dysfunction of the muscles of the eye causes strabismus, heterophoria, and nystagmus.

Strabismus, or "crossed eyes" as it is more commonly called, is caused by lack of coordination of the external eye muscles, making it impossible for the two eyes to focus on the same object. The most common cause of *amblyopia* (also known as "lazy eye") is strabismus.

Heterophoria is the result of one or more muscles of the eye being insufficient to bring two images from the two eyes into one focused image.

Nystagmus consists of rapid, jerky movements of the eyeballs that result in ineffectual vision.

Albinism also causes a loss of visual acuity, as the lack of color in the iris allows too much light to reach the retina. Generally, glasses are prescribed to lessen the effects of strong light. Albinism is a congenital and hereditary condition.

Cataracts are another condition of the eye whereby the crystalline lens or its capsule becomes opaque. Some visual acuity is lost, but it usually can be restored by surgery or other medical processes.

Many other disorders of the eye cause visual impairment or blindness, such as retinitis pigmentosa (an inherited progressive deterioration of the retina) and glaucoma. Blindness can also result from pressure in the eyeball that damages fibers in the optic nerve.

Some people with visual impairment learn to read printed material by using braille. This method was devised by Louis Braille, who was himself blind. It is a system of raised dots that are evenly arranged in quadrangular letter spaces or cells and that are read using the fingertips. Six dots can be placed in each cell, three high by two wide, and 63 different characters can be formed.

Braille comprises two grades. Grade 1 braille uses full spelling and consists of letters of the alphabet, punctuation, numbers, and several composition signs that are special to braille. Uncontracted braille is known as "English Grade 1." Grade 2 braille, also known as "English braille," consists of Grade 1 along with 189 contractions and short-form words.

For many people who have visual impairments, mobility is difficult. Some use a white cane to help them gain useful information about their environment. The use of a cane is also helpful in finding stairs and curbs and provides protection from obstacles from the waist to the feet. The strip of red at the bottom of the long white cane identifies the person who carries it as legally blind.

Guide dogs can be trained to be of great value to people with severe visual impairments. Generally, a puppy is chosen at 3 months old to be placed with a 4-H child and raised in a family setting. The dog is returned to a special training school when it is one year old to receive formal guide work training for 3 to 6 months. The person who will get the dog then must live at the school for 28 days, during which he or she will be taught how to care for the dog and to give it commands. Bonding takes place between the guide dog and the blind person so that they can work as a team. About 1% to 2% of all blind people have guide dogs.

Characteristics

The effect of visual problems on a child's development depends on the severity, type of loss, the age at which the condition appears, and the overall functioning level of the child. Many children with multiple disabilities may also have visual impairments.

Children with visual impairments have normal growth patterns, although those born with the impairment may have difficulty grasping abstract ideas and concepts that depend on visual stimuli. However, if the child's visual impairment occurs after birth, some visually learned concepts and skills will already have been acquired. It is important to remember that there is no intellectual impairment associated with vision disorders. A person's intelligence is not related to his or her ability to see.

The eyes of some people with visual impairment may look different from other peoples's. At birth, a baby's eyes may seem blank or look disfigured. Diseases of the eye(s) also may affect their appearance. Excess pressure in the eyes can cause the eyes to bulge or protrude. Many people who are blind wear glasses. Some may wear glasses for cosmetic purposes only, whereas others who have usable vision may see a little better with them.

Strategies for Educators

Successful inclusion of the student with a visual impairment can be very rewarding for the teacher and students.

The regular classroom teacher needs to provide adequate accommodations for the student who is visually impaired to ensure an easy transition to the regular class. Conferring with the resource teacher and others who are responsible for the education of the student will provide the teacher with information about the student's academic strengths and weaknesses. This information will be helpful in meeting the student's educational goals. Teachers and support personnel should be involved in an ongoing evaluation of the progress and needs of the student.

Although some students with visual impairments may require only a few adaptive materials, others may need special devices. Arrangements should be made to have any special device(s) needed by the student available in the classroom prior to his or her transition from a restrictive environment to a regular classroom.

Book stands make it possible for students with visual impairments to bring their work closer to their eyes and prevent postural fatigue. Public libraries and the Library of Congress have large-print books that are available for persons who are visually impaired. The Library Reproduction Service (1977 S. Los Angeles Street, Los Angeles, CA 90011-1096) produces large-print material of educational materials. The American Printing House for the Blind, Inc. (1839 Frankfort Avenue, Louisville, KY 40206-0085) is a nonprofit company that creates educational materials for people with visual impairments.

The National Association for the Visually Handicapped (22 West 21st Street, New York, NY 10010) has a free lending library of large-print materials that are available through the mail.

Students with visual impairments who are unable to read a regular printed page even when it is in large type may need to use the braille system in order to read. Samples of the braille alphabet and numbers should be given to the students. After having the opportunity to feel and identify the different letters on a braille card, the students can be given a stylus to make their own braille letters.

If the student is not using braille, different types of paper should be made readily available. Because it is often difficult to see the lines on regular paper, bold-line paper can be provided. Raised-line paper makes it possible for the visually impaired student to find the lines by touch and then write on the lines. At times, another student may need to take notes for the student who has a less acute visual impairment. To eliminate the need to recopy the notes, the teacher should provide carbonless paper. This paper allows the one taking the notes to make two copies at once, so that each student can keep a copy.

Students need to become aware of the difficulties inherent in living with visual impairments. Simulations of visual impairments may be done to help other students become aware of the problems facing students who are visually impaired. Students can be given blindfolds made of different materials. Opaque materials can be used to simulate total blindness whereas other less opaque materials can simulate different degrees of light perception. To demonstrate the loss of peripheral vision, the students can use a roll from a paper towel as a sighting tube. Tunnel vision can be demonstrated by looking through a paper with a small pinhole.

Two of the greatest concerns of students with visual impairments are mobility and orientation. This lack of orientation and mobility can be simulated by having students attempt to walk while blindfolded. The teacher should select a guide who will assist the blindfolded student. Generally, a guide who is unfamiliar with the needs of the visually impaired will take the blindfolded student's arm to assist him or her. This procedure is incorrect. The person who is blind needs to take the arm of the guide. This enables him or her to walk confidently and successfully. The teacher should demonstrate the correct way to guide a person who is visually impaired.

Because orientation is a great concern, the visually impaired student should be encouraged to become acquainted with the room arrangement. Once the student is familiar with the room arrangement, it should not be changed unless provisions are made for the student who is visually impaired to be physically shown the change. The teacher can select a "buddy" who can help guide and assist the student. This serves to foster acceptance of the student who is visually impaired and increase self-confidence.

A student with a visual impairment may require more time to complete assigned work. At times, it may be better to shorten the assignments so the student will be able to complete the work. Tape-recording teacher presentations and lessons that the student can re-play can be helpful. Information about assignments and projects should be communicated to the special education teacher who, in turn, can provide the student with additional help in achieving success.

Above all, the teacher should provide a safe and comfortable environment for the student and promote a positive relationship between the student who is visually impaired and the rest of the class. It is important to realize that students with visual impairments have problems reading facial expressions and thus may have greater difficulty developing social skills.

Visual Processing Dysfunction

Definition

Visual processing is the ability to recognize and interpret visual stimuli involving perception, memory, sequencing, and integration. This should not be confused with visual impairment, which deals only with the ability to see.

Background

The processing of visual stimuli is a very complex, active, and investigative process. People with a visual processing dysfunction experience difficulty in visually examining the individual details of an object. They are unable to identify the dominant visual cues and integrate them to obtain meaning from the object. They also have difficulty classifying the object in a particular visual category and comparing the resulting visual hypothesis with the actual perceived object.

The central processing of visual stimuli actually begins with the identification of visual cues. Operations such as receiving visual stimuli, orienting the head and eyes to the light source, and scanning the object are involved in the process of perception.

It has been generally accepted that the retina is an outward extension of the cerebral cortex. Optic nerve fibers transmit sensations from the retina in each eye to the occipital cortex of the brain. Researchers believe that one of the important functions of the occipital cortex is the analysis and synthesis of visual stimuli. If there is damage to the occipital lobes, complex discrimination tasks involving size, shape, and color become difficult.

Visual stimuli processing is dependent on efficient ocular-motor performance. Most ocular-motor processing tasks are closely related to school-oriented work in math, reading, and writing. When there is an ocular-motor dysfunction, it will be extremely difficult for the child to perform the eye movements necessary to scan the perceptual field.

Studies have indicated that frontal lobe damage interferes with the ability to search, scan, or examine objects. Lesions in the frontal lobes may result in "pathological inertia" of the sensory process. This interferes with the motor scanning aspects of perception and the examination of pictures or objects, because of this passive looking and inability to seek out identifying signs.

The processing of visual stimuli at the higher cortical level requires not only visual analysis but the integration and synthesis of the stimuli into a recognizable whole. All these cognitive tasks are interrelated and need to be considered in visual processing dysfunctions such as spatial relationship, visual discrimination, and visual agnosia.

Characteristics

A *spatial-relationship* dysfunction may be caused by damage to the occipital cortex and to cortical lesions in the infero-parietal and parietal-occipital areas. With this dysfunction, the individual has difficulty in left-right discrimination and generally avoids crossing the midline of the body with the hand. There is poor depth perception. Reversals and rotations are also noted in the writing. A child with a spatial-relationship dysfunction will have difficulty assembling puzzles and objects. The identification of a complete form of partially exposed pictures, words, or letters and numbers is also difficult.

A *figure-ground* deficit, considered to be caused by damage to certain parts of the brain, makes it difficult to differentiate an object from its general sensory background. This deficit causes problems in isolating a single word or words on a page. It is extremely difficult to scan for a specific letter, word, or fact or use a dictionary, an index, or a telephone. A person with this deficit also has trouble keeping his or her place while reading.

Visual agnosia is the inability to recognize objects even with adequate sensory information input. It is caused by damage to areas of the brain involved in interpretation and memory recall. This makes it difficult to recognize and name objects, even though the person can describe the color, shape, and size of the object. People who are unable to synthesize visual information must learn to compensate for the deficit in processing by converting the visual analysis to verbal analysis.

People with a *visual-sequential memory* dysfunction have problems with storage and retrieval of information. It is difficult for them to remember the order of letters in a word when attempting to spell the word or the correct sequence of events or letters in a series. The student with this visual processing dysfunction will have trouble remembering the order of days of the week, months of the year, and number sequences. Revisualization of visual clues is also extremely hard.

Strategies for Educators

In the regular classroom, students with a visual processing dysfunction may have difficulty understanding a teacher's written instructions or assignments. If the teacher only presents material visually, the student will experience frustration. When writing assignments and instructions on the chalkboard, when giving other instructions, and during discussions, the teacher should simultaneously present the information orally.

The student with a visual processing dysfunction will benefit from a phonetic or linguistic approach to reading. This does not preclude a multisensory approach, which might also include kinesthetic and tactile methods along with the auditory approach.

The student's difficulty in retrieving information can be allevi-ated by allowing extra time for the student to respond. The teacher should also consider letting the student make use of electronic equipment that allows the student to answer questionnaires and tests orally.

A person with a visual processing dysfunction can learn to com-pensate for the deficit. If this compensation is based on verbal rea-soning, it is important to keep in mind that conclusions based on inaccurate visual processing may be incorrect. As with all other dis-abilities, be patient when dealing with a person who has a visual processing dysfunction.

Much more research is needed to resolve the many questions surrounding visual processing. It is hoped research will lead to a better understanding of the tasks involved in visual processing and more successful educational, psychological, and medical interventions.

5 Other Health Disorders

It is estimated that 0.5% to 1% of all school-age children have some physical or health-related disorder. Cerebral palsy accounts for the largest part of this percentage, followed by spina bifida. These particular disabilities have already been covered in this book, along with other major disabilities. It would be impractical to attempt to include coverage of all health disorders in a single book. However, teachers often express concern over several other health-related disorders frequently encountered in the regular classroom, such as asthma, diabetes, heart disorders, and hemophilia. These are included in this chapter.

Although some health-related disorders may not necessarily impact the student's learning process, they may impact the activities allowed for the student and be a concern for the teacher. Many of the concerns that an educator may have about health-related problems can be alleviated by direct communication with parents of the students and school health professionals. They can provide invaluable information about the health needs of students. Additional information about students can be gained by examining the school records.

Asthma

Asthma is a common health condition of many students. It affects 1 out of every 10 children (Clayman, 1989). Asthma is a chronic disorder that generally starts in early childhood in many cases and becomes less severe in early adulthood. Symptoms include recurrent attacks of shortness of breath, wheezing, a dry cough, and a tight feeling in the chest.

An asthmatic attack can be brought on by a variety of factors, including air pollutants; extremes of high or low humidity; allergens such as dust, mold, pollen, feathers, or animal dander; lung infections, such as bronchitis; vigorous exercise; or emotional stress. Some attacks may occur for no known reason.

Asthmatic attacks can be very frightening to the child. In a severe attack, the low amount of oxygen in the blood results in cyanosis, bringing on a bluish coloration in the face and lips. If this occurs, medical personnel should be immediately notified. It may be comforting for the teacher to know that most attacks pass unnoticed or are controlled by a bronchodilator.

Some school districts allow students with asthma to use a bronchodilator during class or field trips whereas other school districts do not. The teacher should discuss such policies with the appropriate school personnel. If the school district does not permit the student with asthma to use a bronchodilator except in the school health office, it may be necessary to exclude the asthmatic student from participating in off-campus activities, such as field trips.

Because undue emotional stress can be a precipitating cause for some asthmatic attacks, the teacher should provide a nonthreatening and positive learning environment. Although students with asthma generally can participate in athletics, physical activity should be monitored, and excessive exercise should be avoided. When the outside air is of poor quality, it is best for the student with asthma to avoid any outdoor activity.

Certain allergens can provoke an asthmatic attack in some students. When conferring with parents, the teacher can find out which specific allergens might be the cause. The teacher may then be able to take precautions to minimize exposure. In some cases, the appropriate staff can take steps to remove the allergen from the school environment. The teacher may be able to remove specific allergens, such as art supplies, chemicals, or other agents, from the student's immediate vicinity. If the student has frequent absences, arrangements need to be made to allow the student to make up assignments. One word of caution—some students who have asthma may, on occasion, fake an attack to avoid doing class work.

Diabetes

According to the National Institute of Diabetes and Digestive Kidney Diseases (1996), estimates for 1993 indicate that approximately 100,000 children under the age of 19 have diagnosed diabetes. This figure does not include undiagnosed cases, as many children and adults are unaware that they have diabetes.

Diabetes is a chronic metabolic disorder in which the body does not produce enough insulin to process foods efficiently; as a result, there is not enough insulin for the blood to carry sugar to the cells for nourishment. Diabetes can be kept under control by medication (insulin injections) or regulation of diet and activity, or both.

There are two different types of diabetic emergencies. One is insulin shock, which is the result of too much insulin in the blood. Another emergency results from too little insulin and too much sugar. This can result in a diabetic coma.

Insulin reactions and diabetic comas can come on gradually. The educator should be aware of the major signals that are the same for both an insulin reaction and a diabetic coma. These signals include rapid breathing and pulse, sweating, dizziness, drowsiness, and confusion. If a student becomes unconscious, immediate emergency medical treatment should be obtained.

More commonly, first aid for diabetic emergencies simply requires that the student eat or drink a sugar-rich food, such as candy, fruit juice, or a non-diet soft drink. The sugar will help a diabetic who has too much insulin in the blood and will not harm one who has too little. A teacher may confer with the parents of a diabetic student and make arrangements for the parents to provide a supply of sugar-rich candies or drinks that can be made available to the student in the classroom in the event of a diabetic emergency. Often, those who have diabetes will know when something is wrong and will reach for or ask for sugar. If the symptoms do not improve within 5 minutes, emergency medical assistance should be obtained immediately.

Heart Disorders

Heart disorders are also a concern for teachers. By examining the health records of students in the class and by conferring with the school health care professional(s), a teacher can learn what, if any, physical limitations the student's doctor has prescribed.

A heart disorder usually does not impact the learning process unless there are extensive absences from school. Allowances should be made for the student to make up the missed assignments. As with other disorders, some students may, on occasion, use the heart condition as an excuse to avoid participation in certain school events. Because this is a medical condition, the student's doctor is the only appropriate person to determine which activities should be avoided.

Hemophilia

Hemophilia is an inherited bleeding disorder caused by insufficient levels of blood-clotting factor. This results in episodes of varying degrees of hemorrhaging, depending on the type of hemophilia the person has. One male in 10,000 is born with hemophilia. Unless the parents of a child with hemophilia or the school health care professional(s) have notified the teacher, the condition may go unnoticed by the teacher. Thus it is important for the teacher to check the school health records of all students in his or her class as a matter of policy.

Any injury might result in profuse bleeding in a hemophiliac. The bleeding can be either external or internal with no outward signs. If the student falls but has no outward signs of bleeding, he or she, as a precautionary measure, should be checked for internal bleeding by the school health professional. Even simple cuts or abrasions may cause hemorrhaging. It is advisable for the student who has hemophilia to avoid participating in contact sports or activities that could result in physical injury.

A Note About Medications

If medication for a health disorder is prescribed by the physician, the school health care professional(s) will generally keep in close contact with the parents and the student's personal physician. It is the responsibility of school health care professionals to administer any medication that may be required by the student during the time he or she is at school. The classroom teacher should obtain a schedule from the health care professional that indicates when medication needs to be given to the student as a reminder to release him or her from the classroom at the specified time.

Associations to Contact

The following is a list of associations that provide information about the health-related problems discussed in this book. In addition, you will want to refer to Resources: Public Agencies Offering Assistance to Individuals With Disabilities and Their Families, beginning on page 104.

American Diabetes Association	(800) 582-8323
American Heart Association	(800) 242-8721
American Kidney Fund	(800) 638-8299
Asthma and Allergy Foundation of America	(800) 727-8463
CDC National AIDS Clearinghouse	(800) 458-5231
Children's Craniofacial Association	(800) 535-3643
Cystic Fibrosis Foundation	(800) 344-4823
Human Growth Foundation	(800) 451-6434
Juvenile Diabetes Foundation International	(800) 223-1138
Leukemia Society of America	(800) 955-4572
National Association for Sickle Cell Disease	(800) 421-8453
National Center for Youth With Disabilities	(800) 333-6233
National Jewish Center for Immunology and Respiratory Medicine	(800) 222-5864
National Organization for Albinism and Hypopigmentation	(800) 473-2310
National Organization for Rare Disorders	(800) 999-6673
National Reye's Syndrome Foundation	(800) 233-7393
National Tuberous Sclerosis Association	(800) 225-6872
Sickle Cell Disease Association of America	(800) 421-8453
United Leukodystrophy Foundation	(800) 728-5483

Resources

Public Agencies Offering
Assistance to Individuals With
Disabilities and Their Families

In 1990, the National Information Center for Children and Youth With Disabilities in Washington, D.C., listed the following agencies that offer assistance to people with disabilities and their families.

State Education Departments

The state department staff can answer questions about special-education and related services in your state. Many states offer special manuals explaining the steps to take regarding educational placement options for individuals with disabilities as well as providing information about available resources. Check to see if one is available in your area. Education department officials are responsible for special-education and related services programs in their respective states for preschool-, elementary-, and secondary-age children.

State Vocational Rehabilitation Agencies

Each state's vocational rehabilitation agency provides medical, therapeutic, counseling, education, training, and other services needed to prepare people with disabilities for work. This agency will provide the address of the nearest rehabilitation office where one can discuss issues of eligibility and services with a counselor. It can also refer individuals to an independent living program in their state. Independent living programs provide services that enable adults with disabilities to live productively as members of their communities. The services might also include information and referral, peer counseling, workshops, attendant care, and technical assistance.

Office of the State Coordinator of Vocational Education for Disabled Students

States that receive federal funds for vocational education must ensure that such funding is used in programs that include students with disabilities. This office can tell you how your state funds are being used and provide information on current programs.

State Mental Retardation and Developmental Disabilities Agencies

The functions of state mental retardation and developmental disabilities agencies vary from state to state. These agencies' general purpose is to plan, administer, and develop standards for state and local mental retardation and developmental disabilities programs provided in state-operated facilities and community-based programs. They provide information about services available to families, consumers, educators, and other professionals.

State Developmental Disabilities Councils

Assisted by the U.S. Department of Health and Human Services' Administration on Developmental Disabilities, state councils plan and advocate for improvement in services for people with developmental disabilities. In addition, funding is made available for time-limited demonstration and stimulatory grant projects.

State Mental Health Agencies

The functions of state mental health agencies vary from state to state. The general purposes of these offices are to plan, administer, and develop standards for state and local mental health programs such as those in state hospitals and community health centers. They can provide information about mental illnesses and a resource list of contacts to whom you can go for help.

Protection and Advocacy Agencies
and Client Assistance Programs

Protection and advocacy systems are responsible for pursuing legal, administrative, and other remedies to protect the rights of people who are developmentally disabled or mentally ill, regardless of their age. Protection and advocacy agencies may provide information about health, residential, and social services in your area. Legal assistance is also available.

The Client Assistance Program provides assistance to individuals seeking and receiving vocational rehabilitation services. These services, provided under the Rehabilitation Act of 1973, include assisting in the pursuit of legal, administrative, and other appropriate remedies to ensure the protection of the rights of individuals with developmental disabilities.

Programs for Children With
Special Health Care Needs

The U.S. Department of Health and Human Services' Office of Maternal and Child Health and Resource Development provides grants to states for direct medical and related services to children with disabling conditions. Although services will vary from state to state, additional programs may be funded for training, research, special projects, genetic disease testing, and counseling services.

University-Affiliated Programs

The University-Affiliated Programs, a national network of programs affiliated with universities and teaching hospitals, provide interdisciplinary training for professionals and paraprofessionals. It also offers programs and services for children with disabilities and their families. Some programs provide direct services for children and families. Individual university-affiliated programs have staff with expertise in a variety of areas and can provide information, technical assistance, and inservice training to agencies, service providers, parent groups, and others.

You can obtain a listing of all individual university-affiliated programs by contacting the National Center for Education in Maternal and Child Health, 2000 15th Street North, Suite 701, Arlington, VA 22201-2617; telephone (703) 524-7802. Additional information about University-Affiliated Programs may be obtained by contacting the American Association of University-Affiliated Programs for Persons with Developmental Disabilities, 8630 Fenton Street, Suite 410, Silver Spring, MD 20910; telephone (301) 588-8252.

Directory of National Information Sources on Disabilities (NIS)

The *NIS*, published by the U.S. Department of Education, provides information, referral, or direct services relating to disabilities. Although regional and local resources are not always included, it does include nationwide resources. Information about this directory can be obtained from the National Institute on Disability and Rehabilitation Services, 400 Maryland Avenue SW, Washington, DC 20202; telephone (800) 346-2742.

References and Bibliographical Resources

References

Alper, S., Schloss, P. J., Etscheidt, S. K., & Macfarlane, C. A. (1995). *Inclusion: Are we abandoning or helping students?* Thousand Oaks, CA: Corwin.

American Psychiatric Association. (1994). *Diagnostic and statistical manual of mental disorders.* Washington, DC: Author.

Association for Retarded Citizens. (1987, March). *Introduction to mental retardation.* Arlington, TX: Author.

Batshaw, M. (1991). *Your child has a disability.* New York: Little, Brown.

Burke, C. (with McDaniel, J. B.). (1991). *A special kind of hero: Chris Burke's own story.* Garden City, NY: Doubleday.

Chalfant, J. C., & Scheffelin, M. A. (1969). *Central processing dysfunctions in children: A review of research* (Contract No. PH-434-67-761). Bethesda, MD: National Institute of Neurological Diseases and Stroke.

Cicero, T. J. (1994). Effects of patrnal exposure to alcohol and other drugs. *Alcohol Heath and Research World, 18*(1), pp. 37-41.

Clayman, C. B. (Ed.). (1989). *The American Medical Association home medical encyclopedia* (Vols. 1, 2). New York: Random House.

Comings, D. E. (1990). *Tourette's syndrome and human behavior.* Duarte, CA: Hope.

Comprehensive Epilepsy Program of the University of Minnesota. (1980). *Epilepsy and the school age child* (Contract No. 1-NS-5-2327). Minneapolis: University of Minnesota.

Cook, P. S., Petersen, R. C., & Moore, D. T. (1990). *Alcohol, tobacco, and other drugs may harm the unborn.* Rockville, MD: U.S. Department of Health and Human Services.

DeVane, C. L. (1991). *Pharmacokinetic correlates of fetal drug exposure: Methodological issues in controlled studies on effects of prenatal exposure to drug abuse.* (Research monograph 114). Rockville, MD: National Institute on Drug Abuse.

Dorris, M. (1989). *The broken cord.* New York: Harper & Row.

Education for all Handicapped Children Act, P. L. 94-142, 20 U. S. C. at 1401 et seq. (1975), and the federal implementing regulations at 34 C. F. R. at 300.

Epilepsy Foundation of America. (1985a). *Epilepsy school alert.* Landover, MD: Author.

Epilepsy Foundation of America. (1985b). *Recognizing the signs of childhood seizures.* Landover, MD: Author.

Epilepsy Foundation of America. (1987). *Children and epilepsy: The teacher's role.* Landover, MD: Author.

Epilepsy Foundation of America. (1988). *Seizure recognition and first aid.* Landover, MD: Author.

First, P. F., & Curcio, J. L. (1993). *Individuals with disabilities: Implementing the newest laws.* Thousand Oaks, CA: Corwin.

Gillingham, G. (1995). *Autism: Handle with care.* Arlington, TX: Future Education.

Grandin, T. (1995). *Thinking in pictures.* Garden City, NY: Doubleday.

Grandin, T. (with Scariano, M.). (1986). *Emergence: Labelled autistic.* Novato, CA: Arena.

Heinrichs, P. (1992, October 3). Experts slam disabled charade. *The Sunday Age,* p. 1.

Honig v. Doe, 479 U.S. 1084, 107 S. Ct. 1284, L. Ed. 2d 142 (1988).

Individuals With Disabilities Education Act, P. L. 101-476, 20 U.S.C. at 1400-1485 (1990).

Johnson, T. (1986). *The principal's guide to the educational rights of handicapped students.* Reston, VA: National Association of Secondary School Principals.

Kingsley, J., & Levitz, M. (1994). *Count us in: Growing up with Down syndrome.* Orlando, FL: Harcourt Brace.

Luckasson, R., Coulter, A., Polloway, E. A., Reiss, S., Schalock, R. L., Snell, M. E., Stark, J. A., & Spitalnik, D. M. (1992). *Mental retardation: Definition, classification, and systems of supports.* Washington, DC: American Association on Mental Retardation.

Mattis, S. (1978). *Dyslexia. Dyslexia syndromes: A working hypothesis.* New York: Oxford University Press.

National Down Syndrome Society. (1993a). *Down syndrome myths and truths.* New York: Author.

National Down Syndrome Society. (1993b). *Questions and answers about Down syndrome.* New York: Author.

National Head Injury Foundation. (1989). *Basic questions about head injury and disability.* Bethesda, MD: Author.

National Information Center for Children and Youth With Disabilities. (1990a, July). *Emotional disturbance.* Washington, DC: Author.

National Information Center for Children and Youth With Disabilities. (1990b, June). *Epilepsy.* Bethesda, MD: Author

National Information Center for Children and Youth With Disabilities. (1990c, July). *General information about speech and language disorders.* Washington, DC: Author.

National Information Center for Children and Youth With Disabilities. (1992, March). *Learning disabilities.* Washington, DC: Author.

National Information Center for Children and Youth With Disabilities. (1995, June). *Traumatic brain injury.* Washington, DC: Author.

National Information Center on Deafness, Gallaudet University. (1989). *Deafness: A fact sheet.* Washington, DC: Author.

National Institute of Diabetes and Kidney Diseases. (1996, May). *Statistics.* [On-line]. Available:

www.niddk.nih.gov/NIDDKHomePage.html

National Institute of Health and Human Development. (1981, February). *Spinal cord injury* (No. 81-160). Bethesda, MD: Author.

National Institute of Health and Human Development. (1993, April). *Dyslexia* (No. 93-3534). Bethesda, MD: Author.

National Institute of Health and Human Development. (1996, April). Dyslexia. [On-line]. Available:

http://www.medaccess.com.guides/Facts About/Facts_04hlm#P4

National Institute of Neurological Disorders and Stroke. Interagency Head Injury Task Force. (1989, February). *Facts, causes, costs.* Bethesda, MD: Author.

Ottinger, B., and Gaffney, G. R. (1995). *Tourette syndrome.* [On-line]. Available:

http://vh.radiology.iowa.edu/Patient/IowaHealthBook/Tourette/HomePage.html

Pierangelo, R., & Jacoby, R. (1996). *Parents' complete special education guide.* West Nyack, NY: The Center for Applied Research in Education.

Phillips, B. (1993). *Book of great thoughts.* Wheaton, IL: Tyndale House Publishers, Inc.

Rehabilitation Act, P. L. 93-112, 29 U. S. C. at 794 (1973).

Rehabilitation Learning Center, Harborview Medical Center. (1995). *SCI classifications and terminology.* [On-line]. Available:

http://weber.u.washington.edu/rehab/

Role models: Jason Kingsley and Mitchell Levitz. (1994, April). *Exceptional Parent,* 17-20.

Shapiro, J. P. (1992, July 27). See me, hear me, touch me. *U.S. News and World Report,* pp. 63-64.

Spina Bifida Association of America. (n.d.a). *Spina bifida makes them this way.* Rockville, MD: Author.

Spina Bifida Association of America. (n.d.b). *Spina bifida: What the teacher needs to know.* Rockville, MD: Author.

Sternfeld, L. *History of research in cerebral palsy.* (1988, April 4). Washington, DC: Cerebral Palsy Association.

Tourette Syndrome Association. (1994). *Questions and answers about Tourette syndrome.* [On-line]. Available:

http://www.mentalhealthcom/book/p40tourhtml

University of California Office of the President. (1996, March). *President's report* (Vol. 4, No. 5). Oakland, CA: Author.

Van Ripper, C. (1978). *Speech correction: Principles and methods* (6th ed.). Englewood Cliffs, NJ: Prentice Hall.

Vellutino, F. R. (1987, March). Dyslexia. *Scientific American, 256*(3).

Wender, P. M. (1987). *The hyperactive child, adolescent, and adult.* New York: Oxford University Press.

Williams, D. (1992). *Nobody nowhere.* New York: Times Books.

Williams, D. (1994). *Somebody somewhere.* New York: Times Books.

Wolkenberg, F. (1987, October 11). Out of the darkness. *The New York Times Magazine,* pp. 29-32.

Zametkin, A., Mordahl, T. E., Gross, M., King, A. C., Semple, W. E., Rumsey, J., Hamburger, S., & Cohen, R. M. (1990, July 12). Cerebral glucose metabolism in adults with hyperactivity of childhood onset. *New England Journal of Medicine, 323*(2), 1361-1366.

Bibliographical Resources

Aefsky, F. (1995). *Inclusion confusion.* Thousand Oaks, CA: Corwin.

Alexander Graham Bell Association for the Deaf. (1970). *Speech and hearing checklist.* Washington, DC: Author.

Alltman, L. K. (1990). *Nerve protein raises hope for paralyzed: Progress in research.* Springfield, NJ: American Paralysis Association.

American Council of the Blind. (1989, January). *Resources for parents of blind and visually impaired children.* Washington, DC: Author.

American Paralysis Association. (1989a). *The APA spinal cord hot line: A special report.* Springfield, NJ: Author.

American Paralysis Association. (1989b). *Facts about the American Paralysis Association and paralysis.* Springfield, NJ: Author.

Association for Retarded Citizens. (1993, September). *Question and answer page.* [On-line]. Available:

http://thearc.rog/faqs/msqa.html

Banbury, M., & Trice, C. *Mainstreaming: From intent to implementation* (Grant No. G007901295). New Orleans, LA: University of New Orleans.

Better Hearing Institute. (1982). *Hearing impairment in children.* Washington, DC: Author.

Biklen, D. (1993). *Communication bound.* New York: Teachers College Press.

Birch, J. L., & Reynolds, M. C. (1981). *Teaching exceptional children in all America's schools.* Reston, VA: Council for Exceptional Children.

Blanck, P. D. (1994, December). Celebrating communications technology for everyone. *Federal Communications Law Journal* [On-line serial]. Available:

http://www.law.indiana.edu/fclj/fclj.html

Braille Institute. *Are you nervous because I'm blind?* Los Angeles: Author.

Britannica. (1996a, May). *Coma.* [On-line]. Available:

www.eb.com.180

Britannica. (1996b, May). *Diabetes mellitus.* [On-line]. Available:

www.eb.com.180

Britannica. (1996c, May). *Diabetes statistics.* [On-line]. Available:

www.eb.com.180

Britannica. (1996d, May). *Hemophilia.* [On-line]. Available:
www.eb.com.180

Britannica. (1996e, May). *Hypoglycemia.* [On-line]. Available:
www.eb.com.180

Chasnoff, I. J. (1988). *Drugs, alcohol, pregnancy and parenting.* London:
Kluwer Academic.

Clay, W. S. (1995, November). *Inclusion: How should inclusion be defined and why inclusion should not be a general policy for all special students.* [On-line]. Available:
http://141.218.70.183/SPED603/paperClay.htpl

Cleft Palate Association. (1988). *Information about the dental care of a child with cleft lip/palate.* Pittsburgh, PA: Author.

Deakin, D. (1981, June). *The national head and spinal cord injury survey* (NIH No. 81-2240). Bethesda, MD: National Institutes of Health.

Dembart, L. (1988, May 29). Kids on the couch: How psychotherapists are helping children to succeed at the difficult job of growing up. *Los Angeles Times Magazine,* pp. 9-15, 35, 36.

Educational Leadership. (1996, February). *Students with special needs.* Alexandria, VA: Author.

Facts and Services. (1995, November). *Famous people with dyslexia.* [On-line]. Available:
http://www.hensa.ac.uk/dyslexia/facts/famous.html

Feldstein, N. (1996). *Pediatric neurosurgery: Spina bifida.* [On-line]. Available:
http://cpmcnet.columbia.edu/dept/hsg/PNS/SpinaBifida.html

Fowler, M. (1991, September). *Attention deficit disorder: Briefing paper.* Washington, DC: National Information Center for Children and Youth With Disabilities.

Geralis, E. (1991). *Children with cerebral palsy: A parent's guide.* Rockville, MD: Woodbine House.

Getlin, J. (1989, July 24). Legacy of a mother's drinking. *Los Angeles Times,* pp. V1, V6.

Glass, R. M., Christiansen, J., & Christiansen, J. L. (1982). *Teaching exceptional students in the regular classroom.* Boston: Little, Brown.

Greene, L. (1951–1952). *Emotional factors in children with muscular dystrophy. Proceedings of the first and second medical conference of MDAA.* New York: Muscular Dystrophy Association of America.

(Source, year, page)

Handicap News. (1996, March). *Dyslexia diagnosis.* [On-line]. Available:
http://www.inform.umd.eous/Journals/dyslexia

Harrie, R. P. (1984). *What is dyslexia?* Reston, VA: The Council for Exceptional Children.

Health Resource Center. (1993-1994). *National clearinghouse on post-secondary education for individuals with disabilities.* Washington, DC: American Council on Education.

Holland, A. I. (1991, June). *Some thoughts on future needs and directions for research and treatment of aphasia: Vol. 2.* Paper presented at a workshop at Bethesda, MD. Washington, DC: U.S. Department of Health and Human Services.

Hollister, W. G. (1959, September). *A bridge of feelings.* Washington, DC: National Educators Association.

Howard, J. (1994, March 23). Sports. *The Washington Post.*

Imaizumi, S. O. (1990). *Prenatal factors and their influences on neonatal outcome: Identifying the needs of drug-affected children.* Rockville, MD: U.S. Department of Health and Human Services.

InfoWest. (1994). *Frequently asked questions.* [On-line]. Available:
http://www.infowest.com

Internet Mental Health. (1996, April). *Antisocial personality disorder.* [On-line]. Available:
http://www.mentalhealt./dis-rs3/p26e04.html

Kannemann, F. (1994, April 17). Frequently asked questions about attention deficit disorder. *National Foundation for Brain Research.* [On-line]. Available:
http://206.67.86.3/brainnet/attentio.html

Kilbey, M., & Asghar, K., (Eds.). (1991). *Methodological issues in controlled studies on effects of prenatal exposure to drug abuse* (Research Monograph No. 114). Rockville, MD: National Institute on Drug Abuse.

Kolata, G. (1989, December 5). Understanding Down syndrome: A chromosome holds the key. *The New York Times,* p. C3.

Levine, M. (1984, September). *Learning abilities and disabilities. The medical forum.* Boston: Harvard Medical School.

Mann, L., & Reynolds, C. R., (Eds.). (1987). *Encyclopedia of special education* (Vol. 3). New York: John Wiley & Sons.

March of Dimes Birth Defects Foundation. (1989). *Fetal alcohol syndrome.* White Plains, NY: Author.

Mathias, R. (1992, January/February). *Developmental effects of prenatal drug exposure may be overcome by postnatal environment* (Publication No. [ADM] 92-1488). Rockville, MD: National Institute on Drug Abuse.

Meyers, Abbey. (1994). *Serving clients with Tourette syndrome.* Bayside, NY: Tourette Syndrome Association, Inc.

Mother's little helper. (1996, March 18). *Newsweek,* pp. 51-58.

National Center for Stuttering. (1981). *Fact sheet.* New York: Author.

National Clearinghouse for Alcohol and Drug Information. (1995). *Effects of paternal substance abuse.* Rockville, MD: Author.

National Down Syndrome Congress. (1988). *Down syndrome.* Park Ridge, IL: Author.

National Down Syndrome Congress. (1988, February). *Facts about Down syndrome.* Park Ridge, IL: Author.

National Down Syndrome Congress. (1993). *Resources on integration.* Park Ridge, IL: Author.

National Head Injury Foundation. (1992). Traumatic brain injury. *Newsletter,* pp. 8-9. Washington, DC: Author.

National Information Center for Children and Youth With Disabilities. (1988, September). *Down syndrome.* Washington, DC: Author.

National Information Center for Children and Youth With Disabilities. (1990, June). *Epilepsy.* Bethesda, MD: Author.

National Information Center for Children and Youth With Disabilities. (1990, March). *Spina bifida.* Bethesda, MD: Author.

National Information Center for Children and Youth With Disabilities. (1990, October). *Visual impairments.* Washington, DC: Author.

National Information Center for Children and Youth With Disabilities. (1991, April). *Autism.* Washington, DC: Author.

National Information Center for Children and Youth With Disabilities. (1992, May). *Cerebral palsy.* Washington, DC: Author.

National Information Center for Handicapped Children and Youth. (1988, September). The least restrictive environment: Knowing one when you see it. *News Digest.* Washington, DC: Author.

National Institute of Health and Human Development. (1980, December). *Cerebral palsy: Hope through research* (No. 81-159). Bethesda, MD: Author.

National Institute of Health and Human Development. (1988, March). *Developmental speech and language disorders* (No. 88-2757). Bethesda, MD: Author.

National Institute of Health and Human Development. (1990, October). *Aphasia* (No. 91-391). Bethesda, MD: Author.

National Institute of Neurological Disorders. (1993, September). *Hope through research* (No. 93-159). Bethesda, MD: Author.

Orlansky, M. D. (1977). *Mainstreaming the visually impaired child.* Austin, TX: Learning Concepts.

The Orton Dyslexia Society. (1988). *How is dyslexia assessed?* Baltimore: Author.

The Orton Dyslexia Society. (1989a). *What is dyslexia?* Baltimore: Author.

The Orton Dyslexia Society. (1989b). *Where can I find help?* Baltimore: Author.

Ottinger, B. (1995, September). *Modifications for students with Tourette syndrome, attention-deficit disorder and obsessive-compulsive disorder.* [On-line]. Available:

`http://vh.radiology.iowa.edu/Patient/IowaHealthBook/Tourette/`
`HomePage.html`

Powers, M. D. (1989). *Children with autism.* Rockville, MD: Woodbine House.

Redl, F., & Jacobson, S. (1958, December). The emotionally disturbed. *NEA Journal,* pp. 609-611.

Reisner, H. (1988). *Children with epilepsy: A parent's guide.* Kensington, MD: Woodbine House.

Retarded Citizens, United Way. (1991, February). *Fetal alcohol syndrome: Fact sheet.* Atlanta, GA: Author.

Robinson, F. B. (1964). *Introduction to stuttering.* Englewood Cliffs, NJ: Prentice Hall.

Robinson, S. M., Braxdale, C. T., & Colson, S. E. (1985). *Focus on exceptional children.* Denver, CO: Love.

Rosemond, J. (1985, May 28). Identifying hyperactivity. *Daily News,* (Los Angeles).

Rosen, L., & Weiner, L. (1984). *Alcohol and the fetus: A clinical perspective.* New York: Oxford University Press.

Rovner, S. (1989, July 2). America unkind to mentally ill children. *Los Angeles Times,* pp. I3, I26.

Rynders, J. E. (1983, October). *Mainstreaming children with Down syndrome: Cooperative paddling works particularly well when the waters get rough.* Park Ridge, IL: Down Syndrome Congress.

Salzman, J. (1996, March). *Hemophilia.* [On-line]. Available:
http://camil45.music.edu.210/petith/hemophilia.html

Sarno, M. T., & Hook, O. (1980). *Aphasia, assessment and treatment.* Stockholm: Almquist & Wikell.

Shames, G., & Wiig, E. (1986). *Human communication disorders.* Columbus, OH: Merrill.

Silver, L. (1988). *The misunderstood child: A guide for parents of learning disabled children.* New York: McGraw-Hill.

Siporin, H. (Ed.). (1988, Fall). *The L. D./J. D. connection.* Los Angeles: Orton Dyslexia Society.

Smith, S. (1981). *No easy answers.* New York: Bantam.

Spina Bifida Association of America. (n.d.). *Alphafetoprotein blood screening and amniotic testing.* Rockville, MD: Author.

Spina Bifida Association of America. (n.d.). *Emerging issues in spina bifida: Secondary disabilities.* Rockville, MD: Author.

Spina Bifida Association of America. (1990). *Not-so-trivial pursuit of information about spina bifida.* Rockville, MD: Author.

Spina Bifida Association of America. (1990, January/February). *Task force keys on quality health care, special needs for teens, adults: Insights.* Rockville, MD: Author.

Spina Bifida Association of Nova Scotia. (1996). *About spina bifida.* [On-line]. Available:
http://www.isisnet.com/sbans/what__is__SB.html

Stolov, W. C., & Clowers, M. R. (1981). *Handbook of severe disability.* Seattle, WA: University of Washington Press.

Svoboda, W. B. (1979). *Learning about epilepsy.* Baltimore: University Park Press.

Talent, B. K., & Busch, S. G. (1982, February/March). *Today's Education,* pp. 8, 34.

Tanenhaus, J. (1990, Winter). *Computers and Down syndrome: NDSS update.* New York: National Down Syndrome Society.

Tisdale, S. (1990, June). Neither morons nor imbeciles nor idiots: In the company of the mentally retarded. *Harper's,* pp. 47-56.

Truitt, C. J. (1954, October). *Personal and social adjustments of children with muscular dystrophy: Clinical management of patients.* Symposium at the third medical conference. New York: Muscular Dystrophy Associations of America.

Turnbull, A. P. (1993). *Coping, families, and disability.* Baltimore: Brooks.

Understanding learning problems. (1984, March). *Current Health,* pp. 3-7.

United Cerebral Palsy Association. (1989). *What is cerebral palsy?* New York: Author.

United Cerebral Palsy Association. (1993, December). *Cerebral palsy: Facts and figures.* New York: Author.

U.S. Department of Health and Human Services. (1990, January). *Fetal alcohol syndrome and other effects on pregnancy outcome. Alcohol and health* (RP0756). Rockville, MD: Author.

U.S. Department of Health and Human Services. (1991, July). *Fetal alcohol syndrome: Alcohol alert.* Rockville, MD: Author.

U.S. Department of Health and Human Services. (1993). *Fact sheet: Tourette syndrome* (Rev. ed.). Bethesda, MD: Author.

Van Ripper, C. (1973). *The treatment of stuttering.* Englewood Cliffs, NJ: Prentice Hall.

Walton, J., Beeson, P. B., & Scott, R. B. (1986). *Diabetes* (Vol. 1, p. 308). New York: Oxford University Press.

Weiner, L., & Morse, B. A. (1988). *Drugs, alcohol, pregnancy and parenting.* Boston: Kluwer Academic.

Weiner, L., Morse, B. A., & Garrido, P. (1989). FAS/FAE: Focusing prevention on women at risk. *The International Journal of the Addictions, 24,* 385-395.

Weisenburg, J., & McBrider, K. E. (1973). *Aphasia.* New York: Hofner.

Wing, L. (1980). *Autistic children: A guide for parents and professionals.* Secaucus, NJ: The Citadel Press.

Wobus, John. (1996). *Autism: Frequently asked questions (memo)* [Online]. Available:

http://web.syr.edu/__jmwobus/autism.faq